STUDIES IN RECENT AESTHETIC

THE UNIVERSITY OF NORTH CAROLINA PRESS
CHAPEL HILL, N. C.

THE BAKER AND TAYLOR CO.
NEW YORK

OXFORD UNIVERSITY PRESS
LONDON

MARUZEN-KABUSHIKI-KAISHA
TOKYO

STUDIES IN RECENT
AESTHETIC

BY

KATHERINE GILBERT

CHAPEL HILL
THE UNIVERSITY OF NORTH CAROLINA PRESS
1927

COPYRIGHT 1927 BY

THE UNIVERSITY OF NORTH CAROLINA PRESS

THE SEEMAN PRESS
DURHAM, N. C.

PREFACE

This little book contains six essays on the philosophy of beauty. The complexity of the subject, a complexity which seemed to grow under my eyes like the tiny Japanese paper-flowers children plant in a bowl of water, deterred me for the time being from the presumption of a systematic treatment. My best hope for getting a complete vision of the various aesthetic theories seemed to be to "fumble for the whole" by "once fixing on a part however poor." So the present work is confined to the literature since 1890 on the supposition that the ideas of our contemporaries are the most readily intelligible to us, and within that body of material I have selected a few special points and writers for discussion.

Yet I think I may plausibly claim for what I have written more unity and centrality than are at once manifest. I have tried to avoid the mere ingenuities and curiosities of aesthetic speculation, and to aim always at the higher obvious. The problems handled are those we are always at and never done with. The problem of the relation of the sensuous to the ideal in beauty is the theme of the papers on expression and medium. "The paradox of beauty discloses," says Bosanquet, "that art must rise above the actual and remain within the sensuous." The paper on Lalo, a prolific French writer little known in America, is occupied with the relation of personal impression to standards and sanctions of taste. Is the hackneyed saying, *de gustibus,* a final truth or a mere worn counter of discourse? Is there in the field of artistic criticism a parallel to Joubert's dictum about the interpretation of religion, that one should be fearful of being wrong when one thinks differently from the saints? The paper on Croce is concerned with the relation of the arts to Art. Hardy has cast this problem in poetical form in his verses supposed to be written in the Hall of the Muses in the Vatican. His interlocutor is a phantom who seemed to him to be the "essence of all the Nine."

"Today my soul clasps Form; but where is my troth
  Of yesternight with Tune: can one cleave to both?"
—"Be not perturbed," said she. "Though apart in fame,
  As I and my sisters are one, those, too, are the same."

"But my love goes further—to Story, and Dance, and Hymn,

The lover of all in a sun-sweep is fool to whim—
Is swayed like a river-weed as the ripples run!"

"Nay, wooer, thou sway'st not. These are but phases of one."

The chapter entitled "Tendencies and Problems" is my one effort after explicit systematic wholeness. It is a survey of the aesthetic methods in vogue in England and America at the present time. The paper on Bergson's theory of comedy has the most subjective motive of any of the studies. I have long been interested in theories of wit and humor, and Bergson makes out such a clear case for such a wrong conception that he is convenient to start from.

The four title-names, Bosanquet, Croce, Santayana, and Lalo, not only designate as many influential writers in aesthetics, but give at the same time a local habitation to four distinct logical approaches. By taking a variety of personalities and methods I intended to taste around and extend my sympathies and understanding as widely as possible. Bosanquet would have deplored any restricting designation of his method, for he thought of himself simply as one heir of the long and diversified philosophical tradition, a later vehicle of the impulse that moved Plato and Aristotle and Kant and Hegel. The other writers dealt with define their methods with a greater feeling of exclusion. Croce's interpretation is lyrical, Santayana's psychological, and Lalo's sociological. Though I tried to live myself into each of these views in turn, my thinking has never been so plastic, I trust, as to lack characteristic logical substance of its own. It will be obvious to the most superficial reader that that substance has been considerably molded by Bosanquet. Like many other students of philosophy I believe the works of Bosanquet to constitute one of the best modern guides for a person feeling his way in any kind of philosophical speculation. He seems to me at once more subtle and more simple than the majority of thinkers. But there is an important distinction between the expression of confidence and the fallacy of the *argumentum ad verecundiam*.

* * *

These studies have been carried on by grace of the Graham Kenan Foundation in Philosophy of the University of North Carolina, the gift of Mrs. Sarah G. Kenan. The administrator of the fellowship, Professor Horace H. Williams, has long been distinguished for his practical faith in the freedom of thought. He believes both in its intrinsic value and ultimate social beneficence. I have him to thank for the liberal atmosphere in which I have pursued these researches. I am indebted to the Editors of *The Philosophical Review* for permission to reprint in this volume the articles entitled "The One and the Many in Croce's Aesthetic" and "Santayana's Doctrine of Aesthetic Expression," which were published by them in September, 1925, and May, 1926, respectively. My associates in the department of philosophy, Professors Edgar Wind and Paul Green, have kindly read the entire manuscript and have given me many helpful suggestions on matters of detail.

K. G.

THE UNIVERSITY OF NORTH CAROLINA,
November, 1926.

CONTENTS

	PAGE
Preface	v
I Current Tendencies and Problems	3
II Bosanquet on the Artist's Medium	40
III Bergson's Penal Theory of Comedy	62
IV The One and the Many in Croce's Aesthetic	89
V Santayana's Doctrine of Aesthetic Expression	114
VI Beauty and Relativity: The Theory of Charles Lalo	140
Remarks on the Ugly	162
Notes and References	168
Index	175

STUDIES IN RECENT AESTHETIC

I

CURRENT TENDENCIES AND PROBLEMS

The problem which Hogarth himself industriously confuses.—Bosanquet, *History of Aesthetic*.

The energy and diversity of view of English-speaking writers on aesthetics lie on the very surface of our present world of print. For example, Dr. Christian Ruckmick announces that his exhaustive bibliography of rhythm has now reached seven hundred and fourteen titles;[1] and rhythm is only one of many aesthetic problems the psychologists are attacking. Dr. Laurence Buermeyer notes, as he criticizes the position of Mr. Clive Bell, that that position has been capitalized "by a host of writers."[2] And the hosts of the laboratory and the hosts of Bell are but two among several distinguishable groups engaged with aesthetics. The time would therefore seem to be ripe for a survey of these groups as wholes, a tracing of their interrelations, and an estimate of the value of their work. The time would seem to be the more pressingly ripe when the chaos in the bibliography of rhythm is observed, even though the chaos was deliberately chosen for the sake of broader interest, and when Dr. Buermeyer is able to say that Bell's followers "have thrown to the winds incontestable laws of psychology and logic." This overwhelming wealth of dissertation and essay and report about the nature of the aesthetic experience contains much that is important and interesting, but inspected in the large resembles a bright crazy-quilt of opinion, with no beginning, middle, or end, no pattern or direction, no mutual understanding or self-consciousness within its four corners. The first impression is that of a motley congeries of clashing dogmatisms, where the need is for a slow, critical, organic effort to grasp a single theme.

The pressure of analysis upon this body of writing reveals at the outset the widespread conviction that, however much philosophers and men of letters may speculate about beauty, it is the experimental psychologists who will settle things. It is not only the psychologists themselves who believe in their own finality. Mr. Roger Fry, whose temper and training are of a wholly different sort, says that we must probably leave it to the experimental psychologists to decide whether such a thing as a song really exists, "that is to say, a song in which neither the meaning of the words nor the meaning of the music predominates; in which music and words do not merely set up separate currents of feeling, which may agree in a general parallelism, but really fuse and become indivisible."[3] He even suggests that we probably cannot get much farther with the general question of the relation of art and science until the psychologists have settled a number of problems.[4] And in his treatise on English versification, Dr. Paull F. Baum, also of the contrasting artistic tradition, guards himself indeed with scholarly care by reference to the personal equation of 'subjects' in laboratory tests, but at the same time thanks the experimental psychologists for the approximate clarification of the most disputed point in all prosodic theory: the relative importance of time and stress in English verse. And in general he says that "in the future psychologists may, and let us hope will, enable us to comprehend the subtleties of metrical rhythm beyond our present power."[5] What is the method of this experimental psychology to which such primacy of power is attributed?

There is a tendency to suppose that this psychology has no method, in the sense of underlying assumptions or a controlling set of ideas which condition the certainty and applicability of its findings, no method, that is, which a logician might place and analyze. Part of the confidence in psychology flows from the superstition that its abstraction from personal feeling, employment of mechanical recording instruments, and control over theory by a series of experimental tests which are then systematized statistically, enable it to yield pure fact. Thus Warner Brown in his *Empirical Study of Typical Verses by the Graphic Method* contrasts the "deductive and analytic method" which, he says, necessitates working definitions, with his own inductive method which "requires no presuppositions."[6] No one doubts, of course, that investigations may be carried on without any awareness of assumptions on the part of the investigator. But it does not follow that there is no presupposition involved in the way problems are conceived, in the connotation of terms employed, and in the whole manner in which an inquiry is conducted. It seems to be one of the incontestable but neglected laws of logic to which Buermeyer refers that all human theory has a form as well as a matter, that is, a shape and texture consequent on assumptions.

A great deal of experiment in aesthetics, then, has proceeded on the unconscious assumption that the aesthetic emotion is easily available. It is not fair to the best of the experimentalists to say that the method has been: Take any person you please; devise a mechanism for recording his reactions; ask him a question which has occurred to you more or less haphazard but which contains the word *color* or *chord* or *funny;* average up his reactions with others similarly obtained; and then incorporate your result in the general theory of the nature of beauty. But it is true that the reactions of school children and of the only slightly selected personnel of college laboratories have often been taken uncritically as relevant to and continuous with the actions and reactions of the assured artistic mind. You see in a psychological journal such a title as "The Difference between Artist and Scientist," and you find that college professors have guaranteed a group of undergraduates as artistic or scientific, and that then (with the gratuitous warning that we have not here budding Shelleys or Huxleys) certain hypotheses looking toward the universal problem are offered on the basis of the behavior of a callow and undistinguished group.[7] Under the title "The Creative Imagination" you read how children have been asked to make patterns or pictures out of a series of groups of six dots.[8] Whether the problem has been comedy or tragedy, rhythm, melody, or prosody, the tentative solutions have frequently been sought in terms of the choices or behavior of the none-too-sensitive run of humanity. If these are the data, can mechanisms and mathematics digest them into aesthetic theory? Perhaps so; but we surely have here a conditioning postulate and not certainty. It will be remembered that the lady who said, "I don't know anything about art, but I know what I like," received the answer from Whistler, "A quality, Madame, which we share with the lower animals"; which showed clearly enough how relevant he thought the likings of untrained persons were to aesthetic. And Mr. Fry, in spite of his respect for the laboratory, did not call it in aid when he was trying to make his own judgment objective, but tried, as he tells us, to perfect his sensibility by studying the traditional verdicts of men of aesthetic sensibility in the past, and by constant comparison of his own reactions with those of his contemporaries who were specially gifted in this way.[9] And it was this same conviction that the specifically aesthetic emotion is a distinguished spiritual activity, a feeling elevated into a value, not an indiscriminate response, that motivated John LaFarge's epigram: "It is not we who judge a work of art, rather is it the work of art that judges us."

One of the most interesting features of current experimental aesthetic is the growing sense within itself of its own former methodical simple-mindedness. Some of the best investigators, conscious of the weakness entailed by miscellaneous 'subjects,' have been turning their attention from data to donors. What is meant by the conception of the fit audience? they have virtually been asking. Mr. Edward Bullough and Mr. C. W. Valentine, among Englishmen, have made elaborate classifications of persons on the basis of their mode of apprehension of an aesthetic object. One instance of such a classification will serve to show how these psychologists are working. Mr. Bullough places lowest in aesthetic development the physiological type, that is, such persons as characterize a color or sound as soothing or jarring to the nerves. Second comes the non-fused associative type. This includes the people who like landscapes because they remember that they were once happy amid such scenes. Persons of the third, or objective type, fix their attention upon the object and not upon their own experiences, but they are excessively critical and aloof. They judge colors as pure or foggy, tones as full or round. They lack intimacy of feeling and decided preference among objects. Bullough places fourth those who fuse their associations with the object. Among inhering associations are those of the blue of the sky in the color blue and of the green of foliage in the color green. Highest of all he places the character type—those who react to colors or tones as if sense-elements and complexes had personalities. Certain people find orange mysterious or delicate; saturated red, dashing or majestic; particular tones meek or happy, forceful or sullen. Another distinction which seems to this psychologist significant is that between the analytic and synthetic type of mind, between those who grasp an object centrally and as a whole, and those who take it piece by piece or aspect after aspect.[10]

Such evaluation of the testimony of subjects is a step in the direction of criticism. It signalizes the growing recognition among psychologists that the aesthetic experience is not to be tested anyhow, anywhere, by anyone. It shows their own consciousness of the relativity of their experimental findings. The comparative culture, or intelligence, or maturity of the persons engaged is more and more taken into account, and the testimony of artists themselves is occasionally drawn upon. The introspective report of Henry Cowell recently published in the *American Journal of Psychology*[11] is an example. And yet granting all this, it still seems as if the implications of the principle of criticism have scarcely as yet begun to unfold themselves for laboratory workers. If your subjects are non-artists, even if they are of the selected 'character-type,' their reactions and the processes of genuine artists seem well-nigh incommensurable. Consider, for instance, William Morris' exquisite discrimination of color[12] in comparison with the feeling of any layman you know. Or mentally compare the way George Eliot is said to have read poetry[13] with the way it would be read by any one you would be likely to find in an American psychological laboratory, and think in the light of this comparison how much weight you would care to give in a theory of prosody to the experimentalists. One writer of this school says: "Pay more attention to the actual performance of an individual in producing spoken verse";[14] but is not the capacity of the performer as important as the actuality of his performance? And when artists themselves are consulted what guarantee is there that they can report and analyze their own creative processes, and that they do not mingle inference with event and theory with emotion? And what is to be the interpretation of the almost universal *lacuna* in the artist's awareness of his own creative processes? "The closest observation on my part has failed to reveal what the exact relationship is, if there be one, between my musical creations and the experiences which have preceded it, either immediately or remotely," says Mr. Cowell. All these considerations ought indefinitely to complicate the 'scientific' treatment of the feeling toward beauty.

You can state the psychologists' assumption of miscellaneous subjects also in terms of undiscriminated mental function. The attitude of immediate attraction is frequently taken by them as one with the attitude of aesthetic appreciation. Of course, formally, the category of

TENDENCIES AND PROBLEMS 13

'feeling' covers both the assertion of an ungrounded preference and the expression of instructed admiration. But the same words, "I like it," issuing from very different levels of knowledge and sensitiveness may be judgments that belong essentially in different worlds. The aesthetic appreciation of music on its most organic and intelligent level would, probably, show more structural analogies with the mathematical mind in operation than with a vague warm 'love of music.' If this difference in background and composition of mind is important, it seems as if Mr. Valentine took a serious matter lightly when, in the interests of convenience, he substituted for the question, 'Do you find this beautiful and why?' the question, 'Do you like this, and why?' or the question, 'Do you find this pleasing?' He explains the substitution by saying that the question containing the word 'beautiful' too often led to a discussion as to the application of the term.[15] But one wonders whether there is any rational sense in which the convenient questions could be regarded as a substitute for the inconvenient one.

Another assumption that has qualified psychological research has been that of the identity of a sensuous element within an aesthetic whole and outside it, or prior to its absorption into such a context, and after. Perhaps an inquiry into shapes and colors and tones isolated, floating in the void or in an artificially simplified atmosphere, is relevant to an inquiry into their nature when they are embodied in a picture or sonata. It depends on how much alterative power over the parts you attribute to the whole. At any rate, we find pure form constantly studied in contemporary experimental aesthetic under the assumption that such study bears significantly on the actual normal practice of aesthetic appreciation. "R . . . is the most used sound in English poetry."[16] Well?—Beauty in a pure line is expressed by unity of direction, continuity, roundness of curves, lack of angles, and periodical repetition of certain elements, or by a certain symmetry; ugliness by the reverse.[17] This generalization on the basis of laboratory experiments is supposed to bear on the question why "authors used to write about melancholy lines in paintings by Perugina, quiet lines in certain classical schools, violent lines in the baroque art," etc. Does it?—The melody problem: How can a series of tonal stimuli generate the experience of melodic unity?[18] But are successive tonal stimuli the source of aesthetic melodic unity, or is their discreteness forced upon them by analysis?

The critical attitude toward what is whole and what is element, what is form, and what is content in beauty does not come wholly from outside psychology. Mr. Valentine remarks that "of course we shall find great changes in the effects of colors or lines when they are built up into complex arrangements such as pictures."[19] But he believes that after the building up is over, the most striking and characteristic effects discovered in the elements still show, and that the difference in the two cases is one of complexity only. For a more radically critical attitude, there is no inference possible from the artificial and formal laboratory of the scientist's devising to the living laboratory of the gallery or museum; or from geometrical shapes, or colors on a wheel or card, to aesthetic element. On this radical view, the setting of a *perceptum* is crucial for its nature. An aesthetic whole is not, for it, built up out of particular colors or tones or shapes, but is made as a unit and felt as a unit, from which later in a time of analytical leisure, tones and colors and shapes may be drawn for inspection and comparison. When Mr. Bullough emphasizes the importance of the "unification of the aesthetic experience, subjectively as a certain homogeneity or unity of the processes of appreciation, and objectively as the unification of the object by composition, content, or emotional and associative import" to the extent of saying it cannot be over-rated, that wholeness is "the one guiding principle, as a criterion of the aesthetic quality and value of the different forms of apperception"; and when he even calls this point of view of the whole "something of an *a priori* principle,"[20] he seems to be approaching a position which if logically developed might be revolutionary for experimental aesthetic.

It is at least true that if the experimentalists are to find themselves anywhere in the same universe of discourse with writers like Roger Fry and Clive Bell a deep remodelling of method somewhere is necessary. Both groups are large and active, both talk about pictures and their elements, and about aesthetic preferences, and they seem to have a general purpose and subject-matter in common; and yet their respective orientations seem to be worlds apart. As the unconscious foundation of the experimentalists' method, except where a critical regressus is in process, lies the assumption of the

TENDENCIES AND PROBLEMS 17

'democracy' of their field, and the undistinguished character of the experience. Anybody can work at the problems, any sense-complex is material. But for the group of which Mr. Fry is here taken as typical, the reverse is true. Selection is for them the very beginning of aesthetic method. They are philosophically as unsophisticated as the laboratory men, but they have had a training which has made them exquisite. For they are connoisseurs, or disciplined tasters, and are knowing to a rare degree about the detail and technique of choice things. They admit only a few highly endowed persons as having aesthetic capacity, which they define as a special sensitivity to form. The values of the world of beauty are, in their opinion, as remote from those of actual common living as the most multi-dimensional geometry. Such questions as, Do you like this or not? Do you find this pleasing or not?—addressed to an ordinary student would simply not touch the periphery of the aesthetic realm for thinkers of this school. We are well agreed, says Fry, that art is "something other than agreeable arrangements of form, harmonious patterns, and the like."[21] This distinction upon which Fry thinks we are all well agreed is the distinction which

Valentine thinks we may ignore entirely when it is inconvenient. "The question of art begins where the question of fact ends,"[22] says Fry. But it is facts alone, barring such a conspicuous exception as Bullough's *a priori* principle, which the psychologists want. While all the energy of psychology is directed toward correlating the wayward artistic emotion with common bodily and mental habits, and toward reducing the idiosyncracies of the aesthetic temper to natural law, the connoisseurs are pressing theory in the opposite direction, toward the esoteric, toward the perfect apprehension of elusive elements. The language of form is meaningless to the vast public, they say.[23] "In proportion as art becomes purer the number of people to whom it appeals gets less. It cuts out all the romantic overtones of life which are the usual bait by which men are induced to accept a work of art. It appeals only to the aesthetic sensibility, and that in most men is comparatively weak."[24]

Here, then, the zeal for criticism, for the sensitive disentangling of the beauty of art, is a strong wind that carries the ship of theory far. What we commonly think of as a great or precious experience turns into something special or recondite. Extreme refinement of artistic appreciation issues for theory in the definition of aesthetic value by exclusion. Determination for this group, as for Spinoza, becomes negation. "Literalism and illustration have through all these centuries been pressing dangers to art."[25] 'Knowledge about' is erudition, and erudition has nothing to do with aesthetic enjoyment. Associations, whatever their degree of inherence or externality, are banned. Imitation of reality, whether it be the reproduction of trivial detail or imaginative interpretation, satisfies an alien interest, these critics say. Even the portrait of a man "in his metaphysical moment" would link itself with the interests of every day rather than with the symbols of the far world of plastic form. The subject-matter of a representation—what it is about—is always a meaning contributed by the fund of actual experience, and it is therefore irrelevant. The only thing that counts is the sum of the "unexpected inevitabilities of formal relations."[26]

It is interesting to note in passing that this extreme emphasis on form tends apparently to assimilate the various arts to music. "Good painting is a music and a melody which intellect only can appreciate and that with difficulty."[27] Just so for the self-conscious Symbolist poet, Mallarmé, the effect of poetry had to be obtained through musical allusiveness and the abstract cadences and overtones of language, and by no means through the normal sense of words. "A poem must be an enigma for the vulgar, chamber-music for the initiated."[28]

And not only with this extreme accent do the arts move toward the condition of music, but they all, including music, might be interpreted mystically. In this particular phase of contemporary aesthetic the moment of other-worldliness seems to find one of its numerous expressions. In his obscure orchestrations of sound Mallarmé was seeking not to produce a succession of pleasant auditory sensations but to shadow forth a Platonic Idea. And it is some profound universal Idea which masters in paint, according to Fry, are trying through rhythmic symbols to make accessible to the more common human understandings. And these artistic Idealisms have their parallel apparently in the musical compositions of Scriabin, who was "evidently trying to make music not articulate, but suggestive of some vision which tempts and eludes his gaze."[29] His "aerial flights" were

TENDENCIES AND PROBLEMS 21

essays to lead men "through the different avenues of sense to some remote and central dwelling-place of the soul."[30]

In this movement away from actuality, aesthetic theory seems to be thinning out past the limit of intelligibility. Yet a mysticism, however dream-like and exclusive, need not be taken as the assertion of a bare nothing. In spite of the radical withdrawal from life, it seems to me hardly accurate to say that Bell's expression 'significant form' would be more truly described as 'insignificant' or 'meaningless' form.[31] I do think members of this group suggest here and there some content for the special experience. In his essay on Blake's pictures, for instance, Fry interprets those formal elements in which he is interested, the masses and spaces, lights and lines, as "the visible counterparts to those words, like *the deep, many waters, firmament, the foundations of the earth, pit, and host,* whose resonant overtones blur and enrich the sense of the Old Testament."[32] Blake drew almost nothing, Fry says, from external nature, but almost all his inspiration came from the vague and tremendous imagery of the Bible upon which his spirit had been fed. Blake himself described his "David

22 STUDIES IN RECENT AESTHETIC

and Bathsheba" as "the mental abstract of voluptuousness." At times Fry asserts, it is true, that the aesthetic experience involves "complete independence of all the presuppositions and experience which the spectator brings with him from his past life," but at other times he says that for the highest art there is required a "patient and scientific quarrying from the infinite possibilities of nature."[33] At times he is unequivocally opposed to imitation in art; at other times he says more mildly that any degree of representation is consistent with art.[34] And it does not sound like mysticism in the bad sense, the drifting away from all definite significance, when he elaborately likens the artist's mind to the scientist's.

As one criticism makes these connoisseurs vague mystics, another accuses them of foregoing all effects save those won from mere sensation, of identifying plastic form with decorative pattern, of making the figures on rugs or wall-paper the ideal of design.[35] It is true that in practice the extremes of mysticism and sensationism often meet. But we have seen that in this instance something more solid than a chimerical fancy seems to be intended by the mysticism, and I believe that similarly something more significant than pure sensation is intended by the formal symbols. Fry explicitly affirms that the decorators *fail* because they do not know how to distinguish between what is agreeable and what is imaginative.[86] Not the immediately pleasant, but the universally valid in perception seems to be for the formalists, as for Plato, the content of the aesthetic ideal. They often make the universal form too strange and inaccessible a quality of things. Mr. Bell talks about escaping through art from circumstance to ecstacy, attributes to art the capturing and embodying of our "shyest and most ethereal conceptions," calls naturalism "nasty," and when he does not place true formal appreciation on the frontiers of reality advances it over the edge into a kingdom beyond. And yet the metaphysical hypothesis which he explicitly states, and which Mr. Fry more parenthetically introduces, shows a family likeness to a well-known strain in the history of philosophy. At their best, the connoisseurs identify the artist's vision not with the thin ghost of reality, but with "that Universal which informs every particular."[87] Indeed it is not when Mr. Bell conceives himself to be talking philosophy, when he seasons his discourse with references to "the thing-in-itself" and "the ultimate Reality," that he is actually in his best philosophical manner. It is rather when he and Mr. Fry try to give positive content to the essence of visible objects that they sketch in an aesthetic idealism which is worth examining. They seem to be seeking what might be called "the pure forms of intuition," in so far as such forms exist in the phenomenal world. It is as if they conceived their task as the separating out from the general structure of sensible experience those necessary, functional modes of semblances which have an affinity for the supreme excitements and swayings of our human spirit. The wide and deep reactions to beauty are given, they seem to say; where are the wide and deep principles in the sensible universe that cause them? Ordinary practical folk, so the theory runs, identify objects by some little eccentricity, some feather in the hat or mole on the cheek. Great artists, on the contrary, attend to the "universal aspects of natural form" which, being common to all things, are by most observers wholly neglected.[88] The personal, dynamic, rhythmical treatment of these unnoticed omnipresent elements—the elements of line, mass, light, color, space—is the realization of form, and is authentic artistic 'expression.' This is an abstruse doctrine, but it is not nonsense. The claim of the formalists that their adumbrations of the 'Idea,' their symbols and necessary relations, are a fuller and completer reality than any we know outside art,[39] is intelligible if not convincing.

The pull of temperament, with aestheticians, seems to be either into the clouds and out of sight, or prosaically down toward the obvious. One type conserves the value of beauty and of the creative imagination at all costs; the other type is chiefly concerned to see all the facts and experiences of life in their togetherness. The symbolists and formalists and idealists seem to their critics to be so choice with beauty that they attenuate it into an abstraction; but the danger with the critics is that, in their concern not to stiffen a distinction into a division, they may lose the distinction altogether. The cardinal postulate with the genetic school —Dewey, Santayana, and their train of associates—from which we have drawn the critics of formalism, is that no 'value' is special, or, as they say, compartmental. "The aesthetic good is hatched in the same nest with the others, and is incapable of flying far in a different air."[40] The experimentalists seem to belittle the difference made to the aesthetic experience by its preciousness; the formalists make the preciousness all in all; the genetic group dovetail it with the rest of life and nature. For every assertion in Fry or Bell of the disparity between life and art, there is at least one assertion in Dewey, or a sympathizer, of the continuity of the two. "Experience cannot be shredded up and parcelled out . . . : what is moral and religious is not therefore non-aesthetic."[41] Take the phrase 'the unity of the mind' in simple literal earnest, is the teaching of Dewey, and you break down the supposed barrier between common practice and the far reaches of culture and beauty. Take the phrase 'the art of living' as no artificial metaphor, and you will have the vital matrix from which all the separate arts and museum exhibitions are offspring.

What is the instrument of articulation by which this particular group of writers join together that art and life which others put asunder? Their method is the Darwinian one of tracing origins and observing development in the plain historical sense. Their fundamental postulate is that the past empirical career of anything, the story of how it came to be what it is, is the ideal explanation of its nature. Show how a thing is built up in time, and you have given the best possible definition of its constitution, they believe. In the process of *becoming* is revealed the nature of *being*.

Now when in pursuance of this evolutionary method you look for the historical origins of the different mental functions, you find a vague general base of instinct for them all. In the beginning, religion and art and morality and the solution of the material problems of existence were inextricably fused. And so the pattern for a treatment of aesthetic, with this school, is simply the pattern of a general psychology. The spring of beauty, like the spring of other values, is in the vital functions, the natural propensities, the nervous gropings. Your Darwinian philosopher begins his aesthetic with a survey and analysis of the instincts, and he then proceeds to show how the original dynamic stuff is fashioned and refined by intelligence. Certain instincts may be set apart as particularly inwoven with the enjoyment of beauty. Baldwin, for instance, selects two rudimentary forces, the tendency to imitation and to self-display.[42] And Tufts, grounding his theory on the work of the ethnologists, shows how the art-impulse may be regarded as a by-product of economic, sexual, and military demands.[48] But even if there is some attempt at distinction of type near the roots of art, the heterogeneity asserted is slight in proportion to the homogeneity. And this is natural, for biological life *is* massive and simple in its early stages, and if the early stages are crucial for the explanation of late quality, then art and practical life are much the same.

And externally regarded, the development as well as the origin of the various types of mental activity looks much the same. Intelligence refines and organizes any instinctive process whatever. The level of the mental process depends on the degree in which self-consciousness prefigures desirable results, adapts means to ends, and annihilates the sharp distinction between means, taken as not desirable in themselves, and end, taken as pure quietus. But intelligence working in this way is not to be distinguished from art, so the Darwinians tell us. All operations are art, and all perceptions beautiful, when the psychophysical organism is perfectly adapted to its environment, and feels itself to be so.

If at this point some one protests that the essence and glamor of the aesthetic experience elude the evolutionary description, as—to borrow a phrase from Hardy—"June-morning scents of a rose-bush in flower" elude "a clap-net of hempen material," then such an one is simply questioning the very axiom of the genetic school. There is for these thinkers no reserve of reason which will ground a fact more satisfyingly than a plain statement of origin and growth. There is for them no ultimate 'spiritual principle,' no artist's inspiration, no contemplative reason distinct in kind from the practical reason. To appeal to such entities would not seem in their eyes like a different approach, but like the resignation of all method and reason. And to all this cry of 'Don't level out the distinction,' 'Don't miss the intrinsic value,' the Darwinians reply that there is as much assumption involved in holding fast by a difference as in stressing continuity. That is, if you oppose the amalgamation of the practical and the physical with the beautiful, you may have too mean a conception of the practical and the physical. You do not lower beauty by setting it within a bed of biological process, they say; you simply conceive the animal life more appreciatively. If, says Baldwin, you explain the interaction of organism and environment quite mechanically, you obviously cannot make the derivation of the highest functions of mind out of that interplay seem reasonable. But, he adds, you must not conceive it mechanically.[44] The danger of preaching in works of imagination is doubtless real, these thinkers say, but absolutely to separate art and morals devitalizes both. It "makes morality dull, perfunctory, and self-righteous, art undisciplined and parasitic."[45] And so the correlation of art with life must be wrought from the life end as much as from the art end. If you impute more glamor to simple existence, then the glamor of fine art will not seem like an unannounced arrival in the biological series.

Is there not, however, still a problem in method for this group? "Before we proceed to ask what history tells us," says Ritchie, "it may be worth while to ask what history can tell us."[46] And I do not think it can be denied that the farther into the heart of beauty the Darwinians move, the more their instrument of analysis gropes and labors. For instance, Tufts can demonstrate plausibly enough that the making of pottery originally answered to a practical

TENDENCIES AND PROBLEMS 31

need, and that realistic sculpture in Egypt had a religious significance. But to the inevitable question why, even if art sprang out of non-aesthetic causes, it yet availed itself of sensuous harmony in the satisfaction of these demands (and is not this after all the only specifically aesthetic question?) he answers less convincingly. He says, in substance, that at the springing up of the arts, men worked much in groups, and that where there are working groups there is likely to be rhythmic action. Rhythmic action, he says truly, is stimulating and facilitating in labor.[47] I think one has an uncomfortable feeling here that the one significant question has been pushed back a stage rather than answered. And when Santayana allows aesthetic value to high monetary costs[48] and couples physiological breathlessness with the experiences of exquisiteness and awe,[49] I think we feel that the inweaving of art and life is strained. And when Buermeyer compares the methodical search for beauty in the fine arts to a scientist's laboratory,[50] it is not quite clear how he accounts for the equipment of the laboratory. For the power to complete and purify chance expressions of feeling which the fine arts possess, and the ability of the professional artist to "construct crucial instances," is the power of the whole *intellectus ipse,* and that, as Leibniz noted, is not derived from the senses. Neither is it derived from the empirical thickening up of sensation in the process of evolution.

Like the genetic school, the little group of English Neo-Croceans—Carritt, Collingwood, Walkley, J. A. Smith—make the aesthetic experience as wide as life itself. Nothing has so held back the science of aesthetics, Croce says, as the separation of art from the general life, and having made of it a special function or aristocratic club. The roots of art are in our common human nature, and the genius is not one fallen from the sky, but humanity itself. It would be truer to say instead of *Poeta nascitur, Homo nascitur poeta,* for we are all lyricists in our measure. So Croce.[51] And those who think with him are never weary of declaring that "art includes both the *Paradiso* and a child's scribble or a guttersnipe's discordant whistle,"[52] and that to exalt it above the common level of experience and fence it around for the use of a few choice throughbreds, as if it were a specialized type of consciousness, is to commit an initial logical blunder. The passionate breathing of the laboring-man to his lassie, the popular love-song on the lips of every passer-by, fall in the same category with the achievements of Leopardi, says Croce,[53] and such a pronouncement sets the pitch for his disciples.

The Croceans do not achieve their strong sense of the universality of the aesthetic experience by the aid of biology, as Dewey and his sympathizers do. The approach, as we shall observe, is altogether different. And yet there is some external similarity in their arguments, because both draw strength from primitive life. Look at the savage and the child, says Collingwood, how easily and naturally they achieve beauty. "Most children can extemporize verses and songs better than their elders; many of them invent excellent stories and draw in a peculiarly forcible and expressive way; and all without exception are at home in a region of imaginative make-believe from which the adult mind feels itself in some degree exiled. The same thing is true of savage and primitive races. The songs and stories, the drawings and carvings and dances of savage peoples are of an excellence quite disproportionate to the same peoples' knowledge and mastery of the world around them."[54] Art, then, is taken by the Croceans as a universal and fundamental activity partly because it *occurs first,* before specialization of type sets in. And the illusion that art is high and difficult comes, they say, from the effort required of adults to "recapture a more unsophisticated frame of mind." Because art is characteristically the expression of the childish temper, all artists as such, no matter how great or old, always betray something of the child's emotional instability, crudity of outlook, and egotism.[55]

Now though this group and the third group arrive at their fusion of art with life by different roads, the similar emphasis on naïve levels of mind leads to a similar unconvincingness in the interpretation of the complex or triumphant examples of art. Croce holds to his theory heroically. Since art is an identical form running from the lowest to the highest manifestations of life, such differences in expressiveness as occur are quantitative only. All differentiation through quality, superiority of worth, rareness and sensitiveness of soul, which is formalism's corner-stone, is babbling and foolishness to Croce. But the problem is hardly to be solved lightly. Among Croce's English follow-

TENDENCIES AND PROBLEMS 35

ers there is a cautious but unmistakable straying from orthodoxy. Mr. Carritt, for instance, is convinced that Croce's quantitative mode of evaluation fails to do justice to some of the normal deliverances of our aesthetic feeling. Carritt suggests, for instance, that Mariana's song in *Measure for Measure* is not merely shorter and simpler than the whole play, but less great. He suggests in general the test of the comparison of fragments with wholes and first drafts with later ones. "If five books of the Odyssey or two movements from the Ninth Symphony survived they would be beautiful, and we cannot be certain because the Melian Aphrodite and the Abbey at Tintern are quite beautiful as fragments that the lost parts may not have combined with them in beautiful and even more beautiful wholes. The beauty of a whole is not the sum of the beauties of parts into which it may be divided, yet it is often, I think, a greater beauty, not merely different."[56] Is not the distinction between the two felt to be something other than between two sizes or thicknesses, he inquires.

Lascelles Abercrombie, who is less than half Crocean and who yet acknowledges the importance of the Crocean influence upon him, takes a firm stand where Carritt takes a cautious one. It may be a "vulgar prejudice" to believe in "the idea of great poetry," he says, but if so, he is content to start with the prejudice and see where it will lead him. It leads him through a whole book of analysis and demonstration of qualitative magnitude in poetry. Richness and inclusiveness of harmony mark a new kind of thing, he says, not merely more of the same. Lesser poets, infinitely precious in their kind, lack what might be called the strength of compass of their superiors. Only minds which are the highest artistically can enchant without exclusion, can link on one canvas sharpest pain and keenest pleasure and manifold types of artistic effect. "Wherein lies the difference between the fancy of Queen Mab and the imagination of the living and anguishing Rood?" Why is Shakspere greater than Shelley, and Dante than Leopardi? Greater scope without loss of shapely coherence, he answers.[57]

But the tendency of pure-blooded Croceanism is to depress apparent differences of quality in art into differences of quantity, and to show art as coextensive with life. The spreading out and linking together is not accomplished, however, in this case, through the help of Darwin, though there is much talk of the primitive. Indeed, it is not clear how far the Croceans have a right to appeal to what is biologically simpler, for their main principle of analysis is logical. The true reason why Croce and his followers can assert the universal presence of the 'intuition-expression' lies in their definition of it as the logical presupposition of all other stages of mental life. To find the Crocean intuition in all consciousnesses is much like finding space in all objects. All other types of mental activity—thought and morality—are complications of the simple imaging mode of spirit. The Crocean aesthetic experience is really not an experience, but a carefully isolated logical form.

Moreover, like the forms of the old formal logic, it wins its universality at the price of content. It illustrates afresh the discredited law that intension varies inversely as extension. Beauty is so simplified and isolated that it has to be defined chiefly in negative terms. Art is non-moral, non-real, non-logical, non-mystical, non-hedonic. As in the case of the connoisseurs who were chiefly occupied in refining away all alien elements and extraneous interests, so concerning this excluding theory of Croce's there is inevitably a suspicion of emptiness and meaninglessness. A theory of art cannot progress far or give much definite illumination that turns forever around the bare declaration: Beauty is itself, and not other sorts of things. You can deduce a definition of ugliness, as Mr. Carritt does, and make a general application of your definition, but that is about all. Artistic error, or ugliness, says Carritt, "just consists in the confusion of criteria, in approving Milton's verse as edifying, or Shelley's politics as beautiful, Plato's philosophy as charming, or Schopenhauer's romance as true."[58]

Even the staunch Mr. Carritt betrays a consciousness of the possible barrenness of so tight a definition. Unsympathetic readers may complain, he says, that such an aesthetic as this only attains the negative result of destroying false—moralistic or hedonistic—reductions of beauty. He replies that even this elaboration of a negation nets something for a clear understanding of the problem.[59] A negation always has its own standing ground. But is there not a serious methodical weakness here? The formulation of Crocean ideas seems frequently to degenerate into tautology. "To imagine well means to imagine imaginatively: to live up to a criterion contained in the activity itself. The ideal at which the act of imagining aims is simply the ideal of imagining."[60] And Carritt's definition of the comic has, I think, a hollow ring: The ludicrous is the redemption of aesthetic failure. The criticism ought not to be pressed too far, for, as everyone knows, the negative or apparently tautologous judgment may turn up unexpectedly full of content. But there seems to be no doubt that Croceanism is on the whole stronger in denial than in affirmation, a characteristic which suggests something about the depth of the theory.

Our survey of aesthetic theories has seemed to yield little but a war of methods. But if, as we have learned to realize, in the *fact* of beauty discord is no enemy to pleasure, might it not be equally true that in the theory of beauty, discord need not ultimately prevent understanding?

II

BOSANQUET ON THE ARTIST'S MEDIUM

> Aristotle regards soul or mind not as the product of the physiological conditions, but as the *truth* of body, the οὐσία, in which only do the bodily conditions gain their real meaning.—Edwin Wallace, *Outlines of the Philosophy of Aristotle.*

A favorite procedure of Bosanquet's is to start with two contrary opinions and show by analysis that their opposition is superficial only. Unlike face, like heart, is frequently his drift when dealing with what he regards as artificially simple ideas.[1] The voluptuary and ascetic, he tells us, take opposite attitudes toward pleasure, but both alike fail to appreciate the nature of vital enjoyment. The one luxuriates in psycho-physical sensation, the other abhors it; but they share the confused opinion that pleasure *is* the sensation of an organism rather than something solid and objective, in the same class with weather or work. Since Bosanquet does not regard the presentation of a paradox and its later resolution as a mere rhetorical device or personal mannerism but as an exemplification of the essential rhythm of reason, it seems appropriate to throw into that shape his ideas on the nature of the artist's medium.

The two extremes of opinion are these:

1. The artist's medium, being physical, hinders his creative act, which is spiritual.

2. The artist's medium, being physical, does not hinder, or in any way affect, his creative act, because the latter is spiritual.

The first opinion—that medium is a hindrance—builds on familiar facts. You wish to copy a bronze statue in marble, and you cannot reproduce the contour of the hand because the marble, so shaped, would break off. You wish to make a bowl with a certain surface and color out of a given mass of clay, but the texture of your clay will not combine with the required glaze and tincture. Inspired by a sense of the splendor of the *Æneid,* you wish to make it over again in English, but even here in the case of language—the most transparent of all the media—the physics of your material, the way the language has crystallized into certain habits and qualities of sound, sets an obstinate limit to the possibility of translation. From the English clause "and were stretching forth their hands in longing for the further bank" you get a far less vivid picture of the outstretched hands than from the original

Tendebantque manus ripae ulterioris amore,

and a far less poignant sense of the distance of the shore and the longing of the souls. Part of the loss in effect is due to the missing openness and sustained quality of the Latin sounds —*tendebantque,* with its four enduring syllables, and the repetition of the long sound 'or' in the penultimate syllables of *ulterioris amore.*[2]

In such cases as these medium seems to function as an impediment to artistic creation. They seem to justify Shelley's comparison of the physical basis of beauty to a cloud enfeebling beauty's light, and even to erase Shelley's exception of the medium of language. His doctrine that the "materials, instruments, and conditions of art have relations among each other, which limit and interpose between conception and expression,"[3] appears for the time being as general law.

Now in so far as this attitude toward medium is effectual with us, we are obviously governed by the show of dead fixity in matter. As opposed to mind, which seems in comparison to be self-moving, adaptable, elusive, and responsive, matter seems on this view of medium to be stationary and lumpish. Matter does not seem to answer adequately to occasions, and mind with its artistic instinct is full of occasions. It seems to remain heavily inert and undeviatingly itself—the settlings in the cup of the universe, as it were—while mind leads its contrasted mode of existence, all energy, all thrust and spring and resource. Under certain circumstances this quality of fixity in matter may even take on to our imagination the color of perversity. When the heaviness of matter obstructs, as we think, the mobility of our purposes, then heaviness puts on the features of hostility. So the body often seems to us related to the soul. It sets a galling limit to what our will can do. It acts as a blockade impeding the normal effluence of our desires and emotions and ambitions. We have all the imaginative equipment of the singer, but we lack the musical ear. We wish to master some field of knowledge, and our mind is capable of it, but we too quickly reach the senseless limits of fatigue or illness. Schumann's injured hand and Milton's blindness were thus dead lines to activity. The general position comes to this then: the dull mass of matter through which the soul must work itself out—whether soul of man or soul of art—sets a barrier in the way of full flowering. The medium, so far, seems to be a regrettable incident in art, a weight about the neck of the creative imagination.

For two main reasons Bosanquet would not admit this opinion of the relation of medium to expression in art. In the first place, the theory implies that the very existence of a medium—any medium at all—hinders the realization of beauty—any kind of beauty at all. But what is actually true, Bosanquet would say, is that the existence of a specific medium conditions the form beauty must in a given case assume, but sets no limit to the general degree of beauty obtainable. The fallacy is in constructing a tight little circumscribed fancy of a beautiful object, and in then demanding that by some enchantment the object be generated out of a material whose nature is incompatible with the detail of the fancy. For instance, a man plans and projects for himself a house with a clear-colored roof, then orders his builder to cover his shelter with a cheap tile which always weathers a dirty black. Or he wants an arch of a certain type out of a material that cannot sustain itself in that shape. It is a blunder in logic rather than a consideration in aesthetics to start with two fixed and mutually exclusive conceptions, an idea of a finished work of art of a definite kind and an idea of a physical substance from which no magician could conjure such a finished object, and then attempt to combine these two ideas in a single whole. The frustration of such an attempt tells you nothing about beauty at all, but throws you back on the elementary lesson of the law of contradiction. The nature of the English language was a fixed condition of the texture of beauty realizable in our familiar translation of the Bible, but who would then deplore, having the King James version, that it fails to exhibit the genius of the Greek or Hebrew tongue? The flavor of the Greek or Hebrew was proscribed, but not on that account greater beauty. "You can copy a thing," says Bosanquet, "so splendidly that your copy will be more beautiful than the thing."[4] Your medium becomes an unexpectedly fertile resource instead of a clogging impediment. You may be driven by the quality of your medium to extreme lengths of inventiveness, but to say that is one thing, and to say that beauty is in general hampered by medium is another.

Bosanquet's first answer to the assertion, "The artist's medium is an obstacle to free expression" would be, I take it, this: A defined medium may prevent a particular foreordained type of expression; but some kind of beauty is compatible with any kind of medium. If beauty is left free, it will grow in any soil.

His second answer would be to point out the *petitio* involved in calling matter dead. What do you mean by the 'matter' of the artist's material, he would ask. If you identify an artist's medium with the physical and chemical constructions of natural science, you at least are arbitrary, for that is only one among several possible uses of the word 'matter.' But if you do so choose, you are not even then reduced to a conception of matter irremediably opposed to the conception of mind as the self-moving. The notion of inert mass is the "killed and stuffed" version of the scientist's matter, Bosanquet says. It is a popular superstition *about* the matter of the physicist rather than that matter philosophically interpreted. For the very definition of matter for the scientist includes the "working connection within particulars," a sort of equivalent of the scholastic universal. For modern physics the material object is dominated by a "general law of action and construction," and this law, though expressed in mathematical formulae, refers to modes of work, or to (and this is Bosanquet's favorite term) the 'life' permeating and sustaining the elements.[5] And this explicit recognition of an order and connection of parts within a 'stuff' is all that Bosanquet needs in claiming for matter an affinity with mind rather than a constitution hostile to spirit, and for the artist's medium responsiveness rather than recalcitrancy to free expression.[6]

If a physicist feels himself the victim of a sophistry in the conversion of his admission of an order and connection of parts expressible in a mathematical formula into an assertion of affinity with mind and an 'ideal' nature, he will perhaps not continue to feel so if he comes to understand the unpsychological connotation of 'mind' for Bosanquet. Our philosopher is no stickler for names. Like all good empiricists he is after the thing. He frankly admits that he does not know what the word 'mental' means, and so he refrains from applying it to the life of a stuff. "If . . . ," he says, "all that is precious and substantial could truly be fused and focussed in an admitted real, I at least should not be greatly troubled at being ordered to call it physical."[7] All that he stands out for is the logical nature of matter, and by logical nature he means what can be reasoned out as necessary to a thing, over and above what a first look at it reveals. In imputing 'conation' to matter as he does, he quite precisely does not impute a soul in the ordinary sense of that term. "What we want and use of the inorganic world is only its externality. . . . If it has souls of its own, they do not help us, because we cannot communicate with them."[8]

But, after all, it is not the physicist's matter which is in question in the medium of art. Only, Bosanquet would say, it is worth remembering that it is not even possible to call the physicist's matter into court in support of a general feeling that matter is dead weight. He would say: From no point of view can matter be fully analyzed and retain its seeming quality of obstacle to mind. But what, then, is matter as medium of art?

It must always be an element in a felt whole —a whole felt to be beautiful. There is no question now of a place in that world which, according to James Hinton, the scientist pronounces real: "dark, cold, and shaking like a jelly."[9] It is a problem now of the contribution made by a physical substratum to a peculiar kind of pleasure. Matter has become a feature in the life of imagination, an aspect of the semblance of a thing. You might say, quite in the spirit of Bosanquet, that while a beautiful object is, as it were, the 'body' of your pleasure while you are engaged in aesthetic contemplation, the medium out of which the beautiful object was constructed, is the body of that body. What, then, is this further body, in our enjoyment and creation of beautiful things? The clue to Bosanquet's answer may be found in his exposition of "the life of blueness," blueness being taken as the outward showing of a physical substance.

"What I see when I look at a blue thing has unity, and life. Its parts, that is, though varied, confirm, support and determine one another by explicit 'compresence.' It pulsates with feeling, a common tone, which involves the presence of a whole all at once, reinforcing and modifying every part by the simultaneous effects of all. What does a unity of this kind consist in? Identity of ethereal wave-lengths? Not at all.

That may be presupposed, but it will not do the work by itself. Blue is a peculiar 'effect'; effect, I mean, in the artistic sense of the word; and wave-lengths, received say on a photographic plate, are not the peculiar effect which we call blue, even if as a physical cause they were to produce it *qua* physical effect. How do the elements of the effect hold together? What makes the blue reinforce or modify the blue? There is no push or pull between them. They work on each other through their identity and difference; or, to avoid disputes, here irrelevant, through their likeness and unlikeness."[10]

If instead of talking about color, Bosanquet were considering those vehicles of the arts which are solid substances, ivory, wood, metal, marble, his analysis would be of the same pattern. What, he would inquire, is the life of the marble in a statue? Not surely so many units of force or mass, but a play of light among glistening particles, delicacy of texture, and a suggestion of durability and heaviness borne in upon you by the whole statue. The vehicle of the vision is not marble with all the expressiveness ironed out of it, and reduced to the primary measurable qualities, but marble with all its tints and veins and crystals actively present and operating on each other within the limits of a given contour. And all this excitement and motion within the marble might just as well be described as an excitement and motion within the artist's sympathetic feeling. The artist, Bosanquet says, lives, or lives in, the detail of his object, so that his feeling becomes a property of it.[11]

Helmholtz' famous essay on the physical basis of harmony illustrates the difficulty of the problem of medium in music, and exhibits in the concrete the tension between the view of medium as abstractly physical and as beauty-component. He seems to shift his point of view, now regarding his acoustical analysis as saying something ultimate and decisive about musical beauty, and now carefully restricting the significance of his physical and physiological generalizations to the sub-aesthetic realm. He knows that his reduction of the physical basis of concord to rate, height, form, and type of collision of ether-wave is somehow relevant to aesthetics, but he does not make it quite clear how it enters in nor how decisive a part it plays. "We must distinguish," he says, "between the material ear of the body and the spiritual ear of the mind."[12] So what is important in the physiology of audition may never reach the threshold of the perception of beauty. This he notes. And again he is careful to say that the phenomena of the agreeableness of tone, as determined solely by the senses—I suppose he means the physiological selection of simple ratios—mark merely the first step toward the beautiful in music. Still, though he thus makes acoustics but a partial explanation, he apparently inclines to think that after all it independently decides something. And he seems to suggest as the only needed supplement a mystical philosophy of mental mood. He seems at once to acknowledge and deny that discord joins with concord in producing effects; for he makes the distress suffered by the auditory nerve from the 'beat' of incompatible tones, and its longing for the "pure efflux of the tones into harmony," an immediate symbol of the demand for peace and rest of the musical imagination.

Bosanquet would say that ether-wave is not directly a part of musical medium at all, though as physical cause it may determine a physical effect that is absorbed into music. But to be a part of musical medium, the least element must be already in its degree enjoyed, and there is no compulsion to enjoyment in simple mathematical ratios. If aesthetic feeling is for the time being set in the direction of shock or inconclusiveness or waywardness, then the vehicle of such an effect will be intervals or transitions or rhythms, that still have a mathematical equivalent of course, but for which there is no warrant in any *a priori* ratio. The decision rests throughout with feeling, and feeling knows no mathematics but only satisfying sound.

The Bosanquetian argument so far may be summed up by saying that when matter enters as component into beauty, it is matter uniquely defined. Aesthetic feeling penetrates the last recesses of its physical instrument, so that matter in art is not the same thing as matter in science. But if when physical quality or substance enters into beauty, it is *ab initio* a part of beauty, then the question whether it can hinder beauty becomes unmeaning. The determination has become a member, the limitation a capacity, the condition a resource. In working with glass cubes or worsted thrums, says William Morris, the limitations are many and rigid, but the limitations need not fetter the imagination. "You may conquer the obstinacy of your material . . . [and produce] a beautiful thing, which nothing but your struggle with difficulties could have brought forth."[13] The gleaming of the tesserae in the indestructible picture, the glitter of the gold, the wealth of color and softness of gradation in the interwoven thrums of worsted are positive enhancements of effect mediated by negative weights of corporeality. Such an interpretation of the power of craft in the molding of matter is, I think, the heart of Bosanquet's philosophy of medium.

Our philosopher's answer to the first extreme of opinion—that medium, being physical, is an impediment to the divine harmony and fine frenzy of beauty—already indicates the direction his answer to the second extreme opinion will take. If the omnipotential principle of beauty can educate a mere physical condition into fruitful resource and active participation, then beauty would be maimed if the medium were gone, and that being true, medium cannot be indifferent to free expression. But this is anticipating an answer which has not been honestly won. By what process of dialectic would Bosanquet move away from the notion of medium as indifferency or transparency to the conception of it as an element in individuality?

He admits that it is natural to believe that poetry operates in the bodiless medium of pure fancy because we discount the physical side of language. And it has seemed plausible to Croce and his followers to believe that the aesthetic experience begins and ends with imagination uncloyed by matter. The quality of artist requires, Croce says, that Raphael should have had a "sense of design and color" but not that he should have had hands.[14] Everybody knows that sculptors often leave to a firm of contractors the transference of the model to bronze or marble. The architect often limits his function to the completion of a design and abandons its actualization to artisans. And with reference to the 'ideal' character of music one has the famous testimony of Mozart that for him invention was all as it were in a fine vivid dream, and that lively mental images did his work for him.

Such instances seem to support the thesis that the whole reality of art is in the creative impulse, in the motion of mind anterior to the deposited product, in the active voice and not in the past participle. But the moral of the examples, taken by and large, Bosanquet would contend, is actually something else.[15] It is that an artist's medium may be so thoroughly assimilated by his understanding and feeling, its gradations and variations may to such an extent have become instinctive knowledge for him, that the grossness and passivity of it have gone and left only a net-work of relations. The matter of potentiality has become the form of actuality. And you cannot say that the medium has been volatilized in this process of its rationalization and internalization. To say that is, once more, to beg the question whether or not the nature of matter is recalcitrant to and irremediably distinguished from the nature of mind. And in holding to the obstinately unideal character of matter, you neglect the definition of it in terms of the order and connection and behavior of its parts. The fact that a genius or a master-craftsman at the height of his power and knowledge achieves beauty without himself touching "the heavy matter and whole natural process of reality" means not that matter and process are indifferent to artistic genius and masterly craftsmanship, but that they can be infected by spirit and exhibit its structure. The matter of an artist's medium can exist implicitly inside a person's head, and be none the less matter for that.

If, indeed, there were not affinity between medium and design, how could we understand the embodiment that admittedly takes place, be it through the instrumentality of contractor, artisan, or interpreter? How, if expression and materialization be not essentially one, can the latter be assumed to resemble the former? How could you be sure that you played the genuine music of Mozart, when you interpreted it on the piano, if you did not believe that the qualities and capacities of the instrument operated virtually in his ecstacy of composition? If a dramatist's imagination were not furnished with true essence of stage—doors and windows, depths and properties—how could you explain the adaptability of a conceived play to a flesh and blood stage? If embodiment is an utterly distinct mode of existence, if it is, as Croce says, a practical and economic event to ensure preservation and communication, there would seem to be no guarantee or explanation of the belief in the identity of what is intuited and what is preserved.

From isolated cases of bodiless fancy, Bosanquet says, you cannot infer the general separability of mind and medium in art. The fancy is not so ethereal, after all, and body not so opaque. He would also say that when artistic creation is in process and the texture of the projected work still somewhat loose, you can often get ocular proof, as it were, of the organic relation of medium to inspiration. You can then almost feel the conation of the physical substratum, as if it possessed a kind of individuality and provisional capacity for self-direction. If you dye very much, Morris says, you call a vat 'her.' And he describes the almost personal quality of metal or clay or glass as it springs into shape or comes alive in your hands. In the same spirit Milton says that in true eloquence the words of an orator are "like so many nimble and airy servitors (that) trip about him at command, and in well-ordered files, as he would wish, fall aptly into their own places."[16] The well-known story of the composition of Poe's *Raven* doubtless gives artificial emphasis to the quasi-independent but 'ideal' functioning of medium because of the self-consciousness of Poe's attitude, but it accents rather than falsifies a principle. Here, as Poe tells us, the seduction of a melancholy refrain and the dynamic property of the sound "evermore" got his inventive faculty in train and led to the formation of the poetic structure. In many poems, though one may not know historically how the element of medium operated in the poet's mind, one can isolate the distinctive contribution, the irreducible status, of certain sounds. Witness the music of chivalry in

> knights of Logres, or of Lyones,
> Lancelot, or Pelleas, or Pellenore

and, at the opposite extreme of dignity, the sprightliness of the bare jingle in

> Waddle goes your gait, and hollow are your hose;
> Noddle goes your pate, and purple is your nose;
> Merry is your sing-song, happy, gay, and free;
> With a merry ding-dong, happy let us be!

The whole notion that because beauty is for the mind and in the mind, therefore it is not for the body and in the body follows, Bosanquet believes, from a "lean idealism." It is easy to show how essential imagination is to art, but, he says, things are no more incomplete without minds than minds are without things. "Our resources in the way of sensation, and our experience in the way of satisfactory and unsatisfactory feeling are all won out of our intercourse with things, and are thought and imagined by us as qualities and properties of the things." "Complete imagination demands externality. . . . Hamlet as a poem in Shakspere's imagination *is* already a fusion and incarnation of Shakspere's spirit in features of the external world, forms of verse, forms of language; 'ringing words,' as Croce well says. . . . A Hamlet which is less than this is not Hamlet. A Hamlet which is as much as this has sprung from an imagination wedded to the spoken language of England, schooled and inspired by its energy and sonorousness. A poem without its sound, I must maintain, is incomplete as a work of imagination. Shakspere was taught and disciplined by the spirit which lived in England and in English speech. Without this externality there could be no Hamlet. To say that externality as a category of spirit involves a dualism is to say that it is a dualism when the musician's work is interpreted by the full orchestra. . . . To treat this performance as a practical means for ensuring the preservation and communication of an imagined beauty separate from it, is surely the very feeble expedient of a philosophy which finds itself trying to put asunder what the universe has joined together."[17]

We have come out then in considering the second extreme opinion just where we came out in considering the first. If medium is not dead stuff, excluded *a priori* from participation in the life of mind, it can neither be totally opposed to nor wholly indifferent to artistic expression. The more you think about medium and work in it, the more its plasticity appears, the more it coöperates, and rises to occasions, and suggests new uses of itself. Body comes alive and turns spirit, even while it remains characteristically itself. And when you get mobility and capacity in matter, a working connection between parts, then, according to Bosanquet, mind has sprung up "like a tender shoot" at the foot of matter, and the pattern of all antinomies is resolved.

III

BERGSON'S PENAL THEORY OF COMEDY

> Neyther doeth it appeare that the other sort of Jestes is of any grace without that litle bitynge.—Castiglione, *The Courtier*.

Doubtless one reason why Bergson's theory of the comic has been popular is that he agrees with the majority in thinking logic has little to do with laughter. He feels that the spice and piquancy of wit elude the careful schematism of definitions. Intellectual analyses, articulating the zest of fun into some abstract relation, into a patent absurdity or incongruity, do not in the least explain, he contends, why such a relationship makes us laugh. "How, indeed, should it come about that this particular logical relation, as soon as it is perceived, contracts, expands and shakes our limbs?"[1] "Matters disagreeing in themselves" may be the sole occasion of laughter, but where is the good empiricist who will tell why these disagreeing matters "take the veins, the eyes, the mouth, and the sides, and seem as though they would make us burst?" Why should caricatures, bringing together in a single representation the characteristic appearance of a man and the characteristic appearance of a beast, do more than suggest to us some connection of similarity or dissimilarity between classes of animals? Why should there be the surplusage of amusement? Why should Dogberry's "Masters, remember that I am an ass; though it be not written down, yet forget not that I am an ass" engage our sense of humor as well as our faculty of understanding? If we hope to understand the whole of laughter, Bergson believes that we must consider what sort of an empirical body the soul of logical incongruity is mated with, and why the human organism is inwardly moved and warmed by an externally-subsisting contrast. To identify the humorous with the absurd or grotesque or fantastic, with some fusion of incompatibles or distortion of normal proportions, and to allow this mere form of inconsistency to define for us the aesthetic species of the comic, irrespective of particular embodiment or psychological effect, is, he thinks, to trust naïvely to remote speculation for concrete explanation.

Bergson, then, rejects "the scholar's excogitation of the comic" because it seems to him to miss the richness and force of the thing itself. For such barren analysis he would substitute "practical intimate acquaintance" and "long companionship" with the life of the comic spirit and with its individual manifestations. This friendly intimacy is, he thinks, better calculated to yield a true impression of the complete fact and solid effectual reality of laughter. Now in the light of immediate experience the incongruity theory of comedy shows itself to him not so much absolutely wrong as thin. The abstract absurdity must be thickened up with some sensuous matter, and matter of a prescribed kind. The empty terms of the disproportion must be painted in with the positive and complementary hues of life and mechanism, man and thing. "We laugh every time a person gives us the impression of being a thing,"[2]—for example, at Sancho Panza wrapped in a bedquilt and tossed through the air like a football or at M. Perrichon's enumeration of the members of his family as if they were mere items in his list of parcels: "four, five, six, my wife seven, my daughter eight, and myself nine." For Bergson, the human and mechanical, animate and inanimate are, so to speak, the secondary qualities of the comical object.

But this is not the climax of his description. Bergson's intention of painting comedy to the life carries him further than the specifying of the content of the contrasted elements. Comedy may be composed of the incompatible qualities of life and mechanism, but what makes this type of incongruity *feel funny* to us? In the definition of comedy you cannot cut off the amusing situation, out there in space as it seems, with its varied colors and clear outlines, from the engaged mind of the man who laughs. The conception of the pleased individual "shaking both his sides" or, it may be, laughing through his teeth, cannot be omitted from a satisfying account of the various members of the comedy family. The process of reflective concretion moves you steadily inward from the grotesquerie on the choir-stall or the missal margin, the anticking clown and mocking tricks of the stage or novel, to the general unified effect these presentations make on the percipient; for it is part of the being of an aesthetic object—its tertiary quality, if you like—to affect the human sensorium in an inclusive characteristic fashion. And it is this general sense of comedy, the precise way in which it is involved with the mind of man and felt by him, the end for which it is begotten and toward which it is directed in actual history, which Bergson regards as the chief element in the description. Above all, he says, to understand laughter, we must understand its function. Comedy may be woven ingeniously out of warp of life and woof of things, but why are we ever moved to weave at all? What part does the fact of comedy play in the whole economy of human life? What feeling does it satisfy and embody? What purpose do its incongruities subserve? That is the final inquiry, Bergson believes, which clinches our understanding of the meaning and value of laughter.

If then, we ask Bergson, not of what comedy is made, nor how it is pieced together, but what in the last resort it means or intends, what is the name of its "utility and function," he would answer: It means punishment. "Laughter is," he says, "above all, a corrective."[3] It was conceived in the spirit of social discipline. In comedy we rejoice to behold the fitting chastisement of petty folly and stupidity; it is agreeable to us to dash down from the human place the swaggering pretence of the human. "Being intended to humiliate, it must make a painful impression on the person against whom it is directed. By laughter, society avenges itself for the liberties taken with it."[4] "[Laughter's] function is to intimidate by humiliating. Now it would not succeed in doing this, had not nature implanted for that very purpose, even in the best of men, a spark of spitefulness, or at all events, of mischief."[5] "Society holds suspended over each individual member . . . the prospect of a snubbing, which, although it is slight, is none the less dreaded. Such must be the function of laughter. Always rather humiliating for the one against whom it is directed, laughter is really and truly a kind of social 'ragging.'"[6] Here we have it. The church and courts administer the punishment of deadly sins; comedy, the punishment of venial ones; but the principle of censure runs continuous from the one to the other. For Bergson, comedy is practically identical with satire.

I think we tend to feel a certain treachery in this final word of Bergson's. Here is a philosopher who has announced the intention of sticking to experience in his theorizing and of rendering the comic actuality in its fullness. Comedy is to include for him both the object of human laughter with all its colors and characters retained, and the motive to it. Now however much running back and forth between experience and theory there may be in the development of the idea of *mécanisme plaqué sur la vie,* it surely is not faithfulness to fact—so our protest goes—to tell us that comedy is essentially for the sake of punishment. As interpreted by the general sense of mankind, laughter, whatever else it is, is the issue of a light heart, and for the sake of joy. For this general sense of man, the 'nipping bourd' is a branch and not the main trunk of the tree.

If here, as I believe, the protest of common sense has truth in it, and chimes with that reflective common sense which we usually call philosophy, at the same time it is true that in identifying comedy with satire, Bergson merely caps a long tradition. Plato's attribution of the pain of malice to the experience of the comic and Hobbes' famous definition of laughter as the sign of triumph over infirmities simply mark two high points in a persistent opinion. And Bergson's position is substantially supported not only by theories of comedy in the history of aesthetic, but by cases of comedy in the history of dramatic writing. It is conventional to say that while the Old Comedy in Athens allowed personal invective and abuse—

satire clearly—the New Comedy was different and milder in spirit. Yet Alciphron makes Glycera write to her friend Bacchis: "I would give a great deal not to lose the love of Menander. If we had any tiff or any quarrel, I should have to undergo the bitter insults of a Chremes or of a Pheidylus in the theatre."[7] Shakspere's comedy is classed as peculiarly genial. And relatively it is. Yet in *The Merry Wives* Shakspere humiliates the hero of *Henry IV*, and the attitude he induces us to take up toward Malvolio and Dogberry and the Shrew, perhaps even toward Miranda, is not so much light-hearted and sympathetic, as superior and patronizing. Our amusement is not without its touch of sneering. The irony of Socrates is, on the whole, gentle and universal in application; yet his irony has its immediate and particular reference to the vain pretensions of the Sophists, and it is not entirely inaccurate to think of the Socratic irony simply as the derision of these penny-wise-men. "My God," he exclaims with mock reverence, after two of them have announced themselves as experts on virtue, "Where did you learn that? If you really have this knowledge, pray forgive me: I address you as I would superior beings, and ask you to pardon the impiety of my former expressions."[8] Indeed, it is impossible to deny that the comic spirit has been abundantly embodied in cutting satire. If you abstract from literary comedy the punishment of the false steps of mankind, "abuses stripped and whipped," according to Bergson's prescription, the trouncing of stupidity, the exposure of legal wiles, medical pomposity, religious hypocrisy, economic greed, romantic extravagance, aristocratic arrogance, and ignorant presumption, you take away most of it.

Let it be granted, then, that Bergson's identification of comedy with social punishment represents a persistent and potent tradition. Let it also be granted that satire contains an animus which is instinctively felt to set it apart from genial laughter. What is the internal logic of this identification and this distinction?

At the very beginning it is clear that satire and humor spring from different sentiments about the relationship of human beings to each other. In ordinary satire we seem to hold our fellowman at arm's length, survey him from without, apprehend by pure cold process of observation and intellection his blemishes and abnormalities, exploit them or mock them or lash them—do anything, in a word, but imagine them penetratingly and sympathize with them. The Bergsonian comedy demands, as our author himself puts it, a momentary anaesthesia of the heart. How utterly this anaesthesia may "petrify the feelings and harden a' within" is illustrated by Oscar Wilde's tragic tale of *The Birthday of the Infanta*. The grotesque exterior of the little rustic dwarf is the one thing pertinent to the royal child's laughter. It never occurs to her that the odd creature is emotionally susceptible like the rest of humanity; and as a result, while she laughs, his heart breaks. In "laughter without offence," on the other hand, there is either no sense of human participation at all, but mere joy in the formal clash of sensations or ideas or points of view, or else there is the feeling that this particular jest is absolutely catholic. The schoolmasterly spirit of superior isolation apparently animates the one, the holiday spirit, the other. Bergson speaks, indeed, of the necessarily social character of laughter, but this "society" of his is an exclusive parish, so that the principle of the separateness of human beings is plainly adhered to. "The circle remains . . . a closed one."[9] So—at least at the first glance—satire seems to imply a metaphysic of windowless monads, the monads being the laughers, and the missing windows, the gift of penetrative imagination; and its theory of the *alter* to be the one presupposed in the Master of Philosophy's direction for the pronunciation of the letter U, in *Le Bourgeois Gentilhomme*: "The vowel U is formed by bringing the teeth close to each other without allowing them to close: U. . . . Your lips are drawn backward as if you were making a mouth; whence it comes that if you wish to mock someone you have only to say to him, U." The theory of personality underlying humor is different. For sympathetic laughter you must believe in the sightless substance of a common mind. You may smile at the fool, in humor, but you must at the same time feel: "There, but for the grace of God, go I."

Now if the appeal of satire is particular and not universal, if its laughter is the laughter of the censorious schoolmaster or exclusive class, a serious question arises as to its title as a species of art. For the principle of artistic taste is not like the preference for tea or turnips, but like the acquiescence in a mathematical demonstration. The artistic form which cannot claim universality or necessity is designed to appeal rather to opinion or impression than to reasonable feeling. But the ridicule conveyed by satire is notoriously brittle. The passing of a generation, a stout demand for evidence from the opposing party, will break its force. "Fashions change," says a commentator on Butler's *Hudibras,* "the bogies of one epoch become the heroes of the next, and what yesterday was apt and humorous is balderdash and out of date tomorrow. That which we praise in Butler now is that for which two centuries ago no man regarded him."[10] Butler wrote for the Court and the crowd of the Restoration, and gave them the stuff they liked. His scourging of the Puritans had but half justice to support it. What lives of his comic performance is not any social service he rendered or condign punishment he inflicted, but the formal properties of his wit, the manipulation of his fable, and perhaps—as we shall see—an ideal satire. If the value of comedy rested on the propriety of a chastisement applied to a class of actual human beings, Hudibras would be dead, for a proper historical perspective instructs us to speak respectfully if not affectionately of the Puritans. Or who could claim that the merit of Aristophanes is his humiliation of Socrates or

Euripides? In so far as the point of the fun in the *Clouds* is the vilification of the real Socrates, it yields in persuasiveness, for us, to the comic genius which inspired Socrates to stand up at its presentation to make more visible the butt. Nor is the satire of Molière, great as it is, convincing for all minds and all times. Doubtless in Molière's mind Madame Jourdain represented timeless good sense and M. Jourdain an immortal kind of folly. Yet so much a matter of mode is that standard of decorum from which the satirical thrust, as commonly understood, proceeds, that to Madame Jourdain's gibe at her husband: "I should like to know what you expect to do with a dancing master at your age. . . . Do you wish to learn to dance for the time when you have no legs?" we could now quite firmly reply, linking in one the ancient Greek and the contemporary American attitude: "Though hoary-headed, yet we dance."

The instability of satire is a familiar idea and can be illustrated *ad infinitum*. Greater knowledge and a better perspective are constantly changing our laughing scorn to pity or respect or cool insight; for the normal setting of satire is hard and dry, not expansive or self-critical or flexible. Shift the emphasis, enlarge the angle of observation, and the comedy, in so far as it means the humiliation of some particular person or persons, goes out. It is this kind of comedy that Hardy has in mind when, after describing the absurd zigzaging of Tess's drunken father, he remarks that it produced a comical effect, and adds that, like most comical effects, it was not so comic after all. Thoughtful writers, from Plato down, have not only perceived the fragility and subjectivity of the satirical form, but have noted the kinship of comedy with tragedy. It is a common observation that, should the curtain that has just dropped on a comic action rise again, it would disclose a tragedy.

But surely the whole theory of comedy does not rest on such a weak foundation as the exaltation into beauty of the arbitrary impression of a particular blemish. Surely, so the claim of Bergson's party will be, satire at its best is aimed at a universal human failing, and achieves genuine objectivity. The object of ridicule, so the argument runs, is not flesh and blood people, who are always better than their squint-eyed contemporaries realize, but certain abstract qualities, such as greed or cowardice or hypocrisy. And these qualities can be true causes of behavior in persons, though real persons are always more than the embodiment of a quality. *Hudibras,* for example, is not directed against the whole body of Puritans, but against the Puritan, *qua* hypocrite. And the *Clouds* is similarly directed against Socrates, *qua* quibbler. In *Le Malade Imaginaire* Molière claims for himself this extenuation of abstraction: "It is not the doctors themselves that he takes off, but the absurdity of medicine." And there is support for this interpretation of satire in Bergson's own essay; for at one point he distinguishes tragedy from comedy by saying that the former deals with individuals, the latter with types. By way of proof he calls attention to the titles of certain well-known comedies: *Le Misanthrope, l'Avare, le Joueur, le Distrait.* "Even when a character comedy has a proper noun as its title," he says, "this proper noun is speedily swept away by the very weight of its contents into the stream of common nouns."[11] We immediately think in this context of the New Comedy in Athens with its stock characters, its reflection of the spirit of Theophrastus, and its influence cast forward on Latin comedy, of comedies of manners in which artificial modes of behavior are the people of the stage, of satires of nations and professions in which conventions represent groups of individuals, of Ben Jonson's *Alchemist* and *Every Man in his Humor*. Who but antiquarians particularly care at the present time that in *Gulliver's Travels* certain of the Lilliputian courtiers probably stand for Lord Harcourt, the Duke of Ormond, and Lord Oxford? On the other hand, the relevance of Swift's satire to the general human vices of quackery, the abuse of learning, and political fatuity never grows old. Have we then searched out the source of the artistic universality of satire, and its necessary connection with laughter, in this notion of the type as its material?

We might perhaps think of laughter as progressing toward a limit of idealization as the analysis of human nature becomes more penetrating. All the springs of evil in human conduct might be condensed into the one or two or three absolute vices eternally worthy of caricature. Ruskin had a theory that all faults reduced to the two of idleness and cruelty. And in Meredith's *Egoist* the finger of scorn is pointed at a kind of universal form of the bad will—a literary analogue, so we might fancy, of Kant's good will. In this way satires might appear to us in the light of Morality Plays with vices (endued with personal names and stage-costumes) making thorough fools of themselves for our edification. Thus, having purified satire from all possibility of error or particularity of application, we have simultaneously abandoned the real show of life as the material of comic presentation, and people like ourselves —neither wholly good nor wholly bad—as the *dramatis personae*.

But on second thought the process of idealization does not seem necessarily to involve the discarding of the real world and its human inhabitants. In a sense our new comedy is more realistic than direct personal caricature. For the more thoughtful the satire and the more it is the work of the imagination rather than of external observation, the more the exhibition reveals—not to be sure the accidents of existence and the chance examples of an animal species—but even so, the truths of human nature. For the comic artist has uncovered the weaknesses of which man is made. If, as was just suggested, Meredith's *Egoist* may be taken as illustrating extreme formalism in irony, it may also at the same time be taken as illustrating extreme realism. Stevenson tells the story of someone's exclaiming to Meredith: "This is too bad of you. Willoughby is me!" and of Meredith's replying: "No, my dear fellow, he is all of us." Barrie's Sentimental Tommy is, in intention, that same haunting and ubiquitous Everyman.

The difficulty for the theory of comedy now is that, having arrived at universality of reference and having so qualified satire as art, we can no longer laugh. It is a serious matter to attend the exposure of our own foibles and vices. Even Molière's Thomas Diaphoirus, silly as he was, had a better notion of amusement than that, for it was the dissection of another person's body, and not the vivisection of her own spirit which he designed as entertainment for his fiancée. The more general the criticism becomes, and the more acute the analysis, and the juster the chastisement—why then the more ineluctable the relevance of the scorn to ourselves and the more depressing the affective tone of the whole performance. Even in personal invective, as Plato pointed out, the pleasure of superiority is modified by the pain of malice, but in connection with these appallingly subtle formal-real-comedy-morality plays one can imagine for the spectator no amelioration of the pain. The mood that would match the object could only be sober reflection, remorse, cynicism regarding the very structure of human nature. We have tracked satire home, so to speak, and we are farther than ever from the genial spirit we sought. No wonder Bergson says that the more a laugher analyzes his laughter the more he finds in it bitterness and the beginnings of a curious pessimism.[12] If our argument has been sound, the theory of comedy as satire issues, so far, in a dilemma: If comedy is satire, it is either particular and subjective and therefore not art; or it is universal and valid, and then not merry.

But there may yet be a way out through satire to a more satisfactory definition of comedy. What Hegel calls the extreme aridity of satire is relieved in the case of the more resourceful and creative of comic artists by an expedient which we have as yet scarcely noted. The playful spirit, the mood of complete freedom and relaxation which we feel to be implied in the very idea of comedy, is not necessarily wholly expelled by the dominant practical and moral aim of satire. In spite of the medicine at the center, it may show a pleasing outside of fable and conceit. It is part of the excellence of the Aristophanic comedy, it seems to me, that it abounds in baskets swung in the air and cloud-cuckoo-towns and frogs and wasps which divert the mind from a serious tendential attitude. Yet so distinguished a critic as Hazlitt accounts the predominance of Shakspere's poetical fancy over his satire a fault in his comic muse.[18] And of course if the essence of comedy is punishment rather than frivolity and topsy-turvydom, this opinion holds. Our laughter on this hypothesis would be more sound and solid without the elfish tricks and fairy courts, the desert islands and ideal forests, the Malapropisms and nonsense verses. Lucian's auction, Swift's Lilliputians and Houyhnhnms, Cervantes' whole "machinery of dreamed invention" detract on this view from the comic genius of the works in which they figure. But we cannot get away from the fact that what is intimately enjoyed in these works today is not the justice of a rebuke nor the success of a humiliation, but the shell and scaffolding and decorative detail of fancy. The allegories and similes, the distortions and inversions, the quips and pranks, which perhaps originally merely served to pick out and set off a moral lesson, are now almost exalted into the total aesthetic significance.

As the analysis of satire drove us, for the time being, to a conception of it as a formal construction dealing with abstract vices and follies, so the consideration of the fanciful element in comedy forces us, again perhaps temporarily, toward an interest in form and away from the notion of art as representation of life. When the spirit of sport is freed from any practical obligation, it tends to express itself at first in senseless absurdities and fictions and incongruities which have no justification beyond themselves, and no "meaning" except the shock of contrasts they produce and feeling for perverse utterance they satisfy. The simple humor of mediaeval grotesques is a case in point. Everybody thinks of puns as, in their way, jokes, and nobody ever thought, I suppose, that they were calculated to do good or to fulfill a function. We feel release in *Alice in Wonderland* and *Through the Looking-Glass* because every possible normal meaning and proper significance is danced upon and jumbled up with its opposite and because in such a line as

"'T was brillig, and the slithey toves"

there is even elaborate mockery of the very pretence of meaning in language. And when Strauss put sheep in his *Don Quixote* and Mendelssohn elicited a donkey out of the elements of music, what social good was aimed at, or what was punished except the whole normal rhyme and rhythm of art? When you begin to identify the comic with fancy, you begin to wonder if the comic experience is not the formal experience *par excellence*. For at times the joy generated by the extravagances and distortions of fanciful humor seems to have no explanation except the satisfaction of an ultimate perversity. The goal of such humor seems to be to confound the very basis of regular logic, the very habit of meaning, the very instinct for connected content. It seems to have no sense beyond the boldness of its senselessness. And it is true that one strain in the theory of comedy justifies this view of its essential formality, as in the notion that laughter is the result of an expectation which of a sudden ends in nothing, or that it is the indication of an effort which suddenly encounters a void. Thus after long wanderings our argument seems to be coming full circle and to be returning to that simple definition of the comic, initially rejected by Bergson, as the incongruous.

And yet is it inevitable that genial and disinterested comedy should be wholly ideal or wholly transcendent? It is necessary, apparently, that if fancy is to operate playfully with human beings some incongruities should be searched out within the four walls of mankind which do not commit us, in their representation, to any cramping obligation. But as in satire the limit of formalism—the comic Moralities—unveiled itself secondarily as piercing realism, so with the comedy of fancy. The last degree of incongruity is within man himself. In a sense, fancy can create no greater absurdity than the rational animal. And contemplation of the infinite-finite paradox in man cannot give rise to any urge for reform because nothing can be done about it. You cannot by taking thought add to your stature or dissolve away the attributes of mortality. But survey with serene detachment all the qualities of finitude—the body with its grossness and sex, as Rabelais and Chaucer have surveyed it, the limitations of knowledge and perspective that result from our fallible sense-organs, the absorbed conventions of civilization, death itself—and view them against the background of man's metaphysical pretensions, his sense of his eternal hope and calling, and you achieve a picture of the irremediable and absolute incongruity. If the comic poet does not quite say with St. Evremond

> There's nothing new
> And there's nothing true
> And it doesn't matter at all;

he says something very like it. He says, at least, that there is no one who calls himself wise who is wise, and no one who claims virtue who possesses it, and that the juxtaposition of clay feet and golden head on this earth is amusing. It is, I suppose, as Sterne suggests, to afford us a sense of the ultimate humor of life that learned men write dialogues on long noses. And one might add to Sterne's suggestion that that is why bishops ride on asses and philosophers fall into pits.

The height of humorous nonchalance and of the expression of incongruity is achieved by Falstaff, whom Hegel calls the absolute comic hero. Everything moral and serious and finite, everything devised by man in his secret longing for better things, becomes for the genius of Falstaff, not, as Bradley rightly says, his enemy, but his plaything, to be tossed about and turned upside down and indecorously placed for the appeasement of an omnivorous and conscienceless and illogical fancy. Everything that imposes limits and obligations, "and makes us the subject of old father antic the law, and the categorical imperative, and our station and its duties, and conscience, and reputation, and other people's opinions, and all sorts of nuisances . . . are to [Falstaff] absurd; and to reduce a thing *ad absurdum* is to reduce it to nothing and to walk about free and rejoicing. . . . He will make truth appear absurd by solemn statements, which he utters with perfect gravity and which he expects nobody to believe; and honor by demonstrating that it cannot set a leg, and that neither the living nor the dead possess it; and law, by evading all the attacks of its highest representative and almost forcing him to laugh at his own defeat; and patriotism, by filling his pockets with the bribes of competent soldiers who want to escape service, while he takes in their stead the halt and the maimed and the gaol-birds; and duty, by showing how he labors in his vocation—of thieving; . . . and religion, by amusing himself with remorse at odd times when he has nothing else to do; and the fear of death, by maintaining perfectly untouched, in the face of imminent peril and even when he feels the fear of death, the very same power of dissolving it in persiflage that he shows when he sits at ease in his inn. These are the wonderful achievements which he performs not with the sourness of a cynic, but with the gaiety of a boy."[14]

The same quality of comic spirit, though with less magnitude and fertility, is possessed by Granfer Cantle in *The Return of the Native*. He will be "jowned" if he cares for the strait-laced ones who rebuke his levity in old age; he will go horn-piping when he is seventy; and his gay fault of rakishness he condones by saying that age will cure it.

The vantage-ground won and held by such characters is difficult of achievement, and we get relatively few presentations of it. Such humor involves sweeping the whole range of finite fact and inevitable-seeming attitudes of the "world of claims and counter-claims" into a common receptacle and contrasting the entire humbled accumulation with the level of mind on which one feels secure because one no longer cares practically about any of these things— even one's own death. In Plato's phrase, the comic spirit flies all abroad, and disdains the littlenesses and nothings of mankind. If, as the allusion suggests, the temper of humor is close to that of philosophical wisdom, it is also close to that of religion. For the essence of religion is salvation—salvation from fear and the bondage of death, and all enslaving things. And the key-word of comedy now appears to us to be just detachment or relaxation—not as Bergson would have it, punishment or correction—but the ultimately happy frame of mind and hale condition of soul. When we lay down a book of true humor, Jean Paul says, we hate neither the world nor ourselves the less for having read it, but we have recovered for the time being the attitude of children. Any figured incongruity will symbolize the necessary detachment from the normal laws of life and logic, but only the incongruity of the finite and infinite will perfectly incorporate it.

IV

THE ONE AND THE MANY IN CROCE'S AESTHETIC

> I will sing one one-e-ry.
> What is your one-e-ry?
> One and One is all alone, and evermore shall be so.
> —*English Folksong.*

"Beauty is a universal which contains individuals but no species."[1] The English writer on aesthetics, Mr. E. F. Carritt, thus succinctly summarizes Croce's logic of aesthetics. Croce himself sets forth his characteristic position on the organization of beauty under the title "Indivisibility of Expression into Modes or Degrees." He says: "A classification of intuition-expressions . . . is not philosophical: individual expressive facts are so many individuals, not one of which is interchangeable with another, save in its common quality of expression. To employ the language of the schools: expression is a species which cannot function in its turn as a genus."[2] Although Croce and his interpreter use the scholastic terms, universal, genus, and species, a little differently, the two men employ them to the same logical end: the denial of the existence of real classes within the world of beauty. If this characterization of beauty be true, it follows not only that the nature of art is different from what many philosophers have supposed it to be, but, further than this, a significant assertion has been made about the general structure of reality.

The first impulse is to agree with the affirmation, at least in so far as it involves a direct interpretation of beauty and does not seem to imply any metaphysics. Nothing seems truer to the lover or creator or sympathetic interpreter of beauty than the assertion that each work of art or each experience of beauty is *sui generis,* and therefore not generic in the strict sense at all. The attempt to dissect or generalize about realities which present such an impressive front of unity and perfection strikes one as of the nature of a violation or misapprehension. "If we insist on asking for the meaning of . . . a poem, we can only be answered 'It means itself.'"[3] Subtleties of analysis applied to a lyric by George Herbert or Christina Rossetti are felt to be impertinent. Analysis, it appears to us, can do nothing but detract from the full compass of enjoyment which simple abandonment to the unique utterance induces. It seems as graceless an act to philosophize about a moving drama as to analyze in cold blood the character of a friend. The construction of a system of classes and the assignment of a Madonna or a sonata to its proper category jars on our sensibilities. The wrong thing has been done. Sure taste has not been operative. Meddling rationalists have entered a sphere where they have no right to be. "Literature being literature, and philosophy philosophy, you can never understand or account for literature . . . by considering it in terms of philosophy."[4]

This is the instinctive feeling of those who know and love the beautiful, and in its general intention this unreflective conviction is shared by the reflective. That art is always concrete, that abstract intellection can never grasp its individuality—these are the postulates alike of the aesthetic temper and of philosophy understood as the embodiment of the penetrative imagination. It is to this view of art as a universe of irreducible individuals that Croce's aesthetic appears to furnish a special canon. While it is true that Croce explicitly affirms this view in an extreme form, the majority of philosophers, it is important to remember, would concur in the fundamental principle. Even Bosanquet—on the whole a hostile witness, for he thinks that ultimately Croce shatters the unity of the mind—appreciates at its full value the impulse toward simplification and purification which inspires Croce's banishment of stereotyped classes from aesthetics. And Mr. Carritt's approval is whole-souled: "Nothing has so stultified criticism and appreciation as the supposed necessity of first determining the genus and species of beauty. To ask in face of a work of art whether it is a religious painting or a portrait, a problem play or a melodrama, post-cubist or pre-futurist, is as ingenuous a confession of aesthetic bankruptcy as to demand its title or its subject. The true motive of such a quest has always been the discovery of rules and canons which shall save us the trouble of a candid impression. . . . The result has always been sterility and dullness."[5]

Croce does not mean to imply by his denial of the reality of artistic kinds and classes that there is no sense in which distinctions can be drawn between groups of artistic forms. His contention is merely that such divisions have no philosophical value: they are arbitrary groupings for practical purposes. Of course, the mere fact of the differentiation of art testifies to some end subserved, however subjective or transient that service may be. He compares the process of classification in art to the arrangement of books on shelves according to size and publisher—an ordering that has nothing to do with the vital matter of content, but satisfies the slight requirements of external appearance and convenience. What he denies is not the existence of artistic specification but its ontological validity. He says in effect that those who wish to talk of epic and lyric, battle-piece and genre, civil and ecclesiastical architecture, are welcome to their vocables and devices, but that they must not confuse their practical activity with the true labor of aesthetic. "Sublime (or comic, tragic, humorous, etc.) is *everything* that is or shall be so *called* by those who have employed or shall employ these words."[6] It is obvious to what intellectual battle-field Croce carries his ideas when he converts them into mere labels. He is a mediaeval nominalist in respect to aesthetic conceptions.

Croce directs two main arguments against the reality of artistic species. In the first place, he can point to experience and indicate the actual failure of attempts at classification. For example, two people discuss the same picture. One calls it realistic, the other symbolic. In any given case they may both be right, for they may mean different things by the same word. And in attempting to pigeon-hole poets, historians have differed hopelessly among themselves. Here is Ariosto, who "appears now among the cultivators of the Latin poetry of the Renaissance, now among the authors of the first Latin satires, now among those of the first comedies, now among those who brought the poem of chivalry to perfection."[7] Yet these various Ariostos are the same person. Again, experience shows the absurdities of finesse of those logicians whose chief interest is in fixing the type of a poem or picture. Not content with the class 'eclogue' to mark off poems of country life, they must sub-divide eclogue into pastoral, piscatorial, and military, however insignificant the works corresponding to some of these heads may be. By thus calling attention to the inadequacy or artificiality of the historic attempts to organize art, Croce undertakes to demonstrate the essential futility of the process.

But in the second place he supports his polemic by deeper-lying reasons. The very nature of art precludes the sectioning of its substance. Art is spirit; spirit is single and indivisible. The tendency to cut up pure act, which art is, flows from the unwarranted application to spirit of a method suitable to matter. How could one hope to frame an abstract classification consonant to the inner reality of a vision? The question has only to be put to answer itself. It is true that the vision is always externally expressed and thus achieves a body. It would seem that the tendency of scholars to classify artistic forms is the result of a confusion of the legitimate consideration of the parts and types of the body with the illegitimate consideration of the vital soul. The intuition of beauty is itself and nothing else; itself is its final category; but the physical fact to which the intuition is confided for safe keeping and communication can be divided and sub-divided. In the painted surface one can distinguish groups and curves of line, hues with their shades and tints; in the poem, strophes, verses, feet, syllables; in a novel, chapters, paragraphs, periods, phrases, words. But this incorporation of an intuition bears a wholly external relation to the intuition proper: there is no inference from the one to the other. Croce believes that the confusion between these two aspects of beauty is the secret of the fallacy of classification. When the distinction between the essential moment of art—the pure spiritual act—and the practical embodiment of art in a physical medium is once grasped, then, according to our writer, the tendency to create artistic species ceases.

In reply to Croce's first argument one may say that failure in the application of a principle does not in itself refute the principle, although a large number of such failures might be regarded as a significant symptom of some constitutional weakness in the theory. But logically a believer in the inner differentiation of art and beauty may fully agree with the charge of artificiality in most actual classification and yet hold to his main doctrine. Old Laocoöns may become outworn, new Laocoöns be written and in their turn need revision, and at the same time the theme of the boundaries and characteristics of the arts be of perennial interest to the intelligence. Thus when Croce complains of the fruitlessness of the attempts to define romanticism and classicism, and asserts that when we fix our attention on the works of the masters, "we see the contest disappear in the distance and find ourselves unable to call the great portions of these works romantic or classic or representative, because they are both classic and romantic, feelings and representations,"[8] or when he delivers the opinion that "epic and lyric, or drama and lyric, are scholastic divisions,"[9] we are inclined both to agree and to demur. Despite the unfortunate tendency to formalism in human thinking which has often prevented the free flowering of the theoretic impulse, periods of barrenness and occasional failures have not destroyed the force of the original impulse. Honest attempts to understand, even if unproductive, testify to resourcefulness and therefore vitality in the implied dynamic principle.

The direction which the process of criticism must take in classifying artistic elements or species is, I think, correctly indicated by Mr. Carritt's treatment of the sublime.[10] After reviewing the contradictions and cross-distinctions in the series of definitions given by Longinus, Kant, Hegel, A. C. Bradley, Wordsworth, and Payne Knight, he feels constrained to agree with Croce that the concept of sublimity is without philosophic value. "Surely," he says, "we cannot resist concluding from all this that 'sublimity' is only a little worthier of scientific respect than any vague interjection expressing aesthetic approval."[11] But a close look at the method pursued by Carritt in shattering the concept affects one's opinion of the relevance—the logical direction and issue—of the conclusion. How does he demonstrate the futility of the idea of the sublime? By testing the notion in the light of the particular examples subsumed under the class-name. In the process of testing he finds a repeated lack of correspondence between specific case and general definition. What he looks for is the presence or absence of asserted differentiae in the concrete illustration. Because he finds some one or two or three differentiae missing in most presentations which are declared to be typical of sublimity, he infers the merely instrumental nature of the idea. Now the chaos in this attempt at aesthetic classification is obviously a fact not to be neglected. Revision at least of the definition of the sublime is called for. But that after Mr. Carritt has announced his agreement with Croce, he himself should actually proceed to revise rather than to discard the term seems to me very suggestive. He does not virtually, although he does nominally treat the term 'sublime' as a mere vocable and device. He works out for the

CROCE'S AESTHETIC 99

concept under consideration an intrinsic and objective meaning, but a meaning far more elastic and philosophical—less mechanical and external—than those he rejects. The word refers, he concludes, to depth of aesthetic experience, and depth he explains as meaning power to overcome the "apparent recalcitrancy of the elements taken up. . . . When the spirit through its expressive activity conquers for free contemplation those obscure and mastering impulses which actually repel aesthetic treatment and cling to their ugliness, then the resulting beauty has a poignancy, a depth or richness, resonant of the discords that have been resolved in it, and we experience preëminently that 'exaltation and even rapture,' that joy of battle which has given rise to the name sublime."[12]

The movement of Mr. Carritt's argument seems to me to point an interesting moral for logical theory. He tends to sympathize with Croce's assertion that beauty is a universal which contains individuals but no species, but he himself reasons in the spirit of that assertion only so long as he treats a species of beauty as embodied in a self-contained formula, and examples of the species as self-sufficient particular cases, and so long as he looks for a point for point coincidence between the two. A persistent lack of coincidence shakes his faith in the objectivity of the concept. At the same time a sure feeling for a true intention in the term makes him instructively inconsistent. What he asserts finally, if I understand him correctly, is that the word sublimity marks, not an exclusive circle of aesthetic cases, but the degree of development of a continuous function. It refers to a modality of behavior within the individuality of beauty, a degree of the actuality of its principle, rather than to a sharply sundered kind of beauty. The transformation that the definition of sublimity undergoes in Mr. Carritt's thought is typical of the transformation that any definition of a spiritual reality undergoes when analysis becomes more penetrating. The farther one gets into the nature of a universal such as beauty, the more difficult it is to match idea with visible and tangible instance. Mr. Carritt seems to have felt this strain of beauty toward the ideal realm, and the relative unsatisfactoriness even for the understanding of beauty of the cave of images and shadows. He appears finally to have tried to put himself at the heart of the universal itself, at the center of the expressive operation of beauty, and to have observed how its own nature forces it to grow and branch and to exhibit varying degrees of power and characteristic quality. In this better kind of defining, the apparent vagueness is due to the greater sense of relativity; there is a clearer consciousness of the reservations under which the defining is done. The task has become logically more complex; there is less reference to immediate sensation, and there is less show of finality in the achievement. Sublimity, for example, when defined as a level or power of beauty can be less neatly labelled than sublimity regarded as a separable and distinct part of beauty. Its definition in the former case must draw more largely from the original definition of beauty, for the species is a direction or intension of its genus rather than a division of it. Again, sublimity regarded as depth of aesthetic experience is less capable of exhaustion in presentation than sublimity defined, for instance, as that which excites specific feelings of repulsion and expansion. Not only is the species felt in the more penetrating definition to be but relatively independent of the universal; the examples under the species are felt to be but relative manifestations of the specific nature.[18] The pressure of the reality of the whole spirit of sublimity is felt but not caught within the particular case.

This analysis of a semi-Crocean treatment of an aesthetic species helps forward the consideration of Croce's own second argument against classes of beauty. That argument is more serious than the first, for it is based not on historical success or failure, but on logical structure. Reality is such, it reads, that art cannot be subdivided. The question is now of the constitution of reality as exhibited in art. When Croce makes the rhetorical inquiry, implying as he does so a theory of spiritual reality and of logical procedure, "Who will ever logically determine the dividing line between the comic and the non-comic, between laughter and smiles, between smiling and gravity, or cut the ever varying continuum into which life melts into clearly divided parts?"[14] the answer is a foregone conclusion. Nobody will, of course. But the true answer to such an inquiry is an allegation of *petitio* and the demand for a critical regress on the assumption of the question. Suppose, instead of inquiring, who will determine a dividing-line, who will cut into clearly divided parts, one inquired, who will make intelligible that pervasive strain in human nature and in art that we call comic? Then the distinction asked for is no longer in terms of a segmented line or Euler's diagrams, but in terms of characteristics or intensions more or less embodied in the concrete instance: and this time a negative answer is not so readily forthcoming. The comic is inherent in reality, truly and objectively, not however so much in the sense of coëxtensive with particular cases as in the sense of adjectival of life as a whole. Life has its comic side which is more or less clearly expressed in isolable comedies. The analogy of the moral sphere is illuminating. We speak of good men. But it has been truly said: There is none good but one, that is, God. Is doubt thereby cast on the objective status of human goodness? Rather we feel that goodness is a virtuality—a Platonic Idea, if you will—which is more or less incarnate in created creatures, never wholly absent, never wholly present. Again it is easier to determine who breaks the law than who is moral. And yet any one would say that the one of these categories which can be more easily connected with a set of given phenomena is the less comprehensively constitutive of reality. Again it is easier to determine what people go to church than to say who is religious and what religion is, but almost nobody doubts that religion is a reality, and a more significant one than church-going.

If one can assert of any world—the world of beauty, for instance—that it is a universal without species and with individuals only, it follows that one can assert that a world can exist which has no sorts or characters, but cases only. This sets in sharp relief the ultimate problem of the one and many. Now the individuals within a world are members of that world, and if members, then representatives of the whole to which they belong, claiming kinship and title by virtue of some characteristic. Croce appears to deny that cases under a universal are members of a world. But his denial has disastrous consequences for the nature of the consideration he is able to give to particular examples of art. It forces him into a formalism in logic such as he theoretically abhors, and it illustrates with peculiar vividness the aphorism that a reformer is usually deep-dyed with that which he seeks to reform. Since aesthetic experiences constitute for Croce an adjectiveless universe, and since no concrete process of analysis can take place where no specification exists, beauty consists for him of a sum of self-sufficient entities, each one an unanalyzable expression; and the work of criticism reduces itself for him to the determination of a bare identity. "The whole criticism of art," he says, "can be reduced to this briefest proposition, 'There is a work of art a,' with the corresponding negative: 'There is not a work of art b.'"[15] It is true that there has been much futile classification in the treatment of art, but it is one thing to find the trifling division of eclogue into pastoral, piscatorial, and military an example of the folly of logic-chopping and quite another to say that there is no meaning in the distinctions of medium or in the excellence of craftsmanship. The line should be drawn not between classification but within the realm of classification between the valuable and the worthless. But Croce by his mechanical treatment of the relation of the one and many in art is forced to the position that individual poems or statues are incomparable except quantitatively. Perfect works of art, he says, have but one quality. "The beautiful does not possess degrees, for there is no conceiving a more beautiful, that is, an expressive that is more expressive, an adequate that is more adequate."[16]

If some one should say that Croce gives a concrete meaning to beauty by defining it as expression, the answer is that his definition, in strict logic, is not a synthetic judgment. The word 'expression' in the context of his treatment does not enrich the term 'beauty.' It is simply an alternative title for a group of facts. When one utterance, as utterance, is as good as any other, the word loses import, for import depends on variety of manifestation in the concrete. Beauty is then for Croce devoid of assignable meaning or objectivity, unique, unanalyzable, incomparable, incommunicable. Examples of beauty are not spiritual functions of a fundamental principle in reality, but mutually repellent units, beauty-atoms. There are, he says, no specific differences between works of art, and no differences of intensity. The distinctions are of extensity only. We have our unit—the intuition-expression—and the science of aesthetics consists in a knowledge of the distribution of units. As in physiology a cell is the unit and the body an aggregate of these units; as in chemistry the atom is the unit, and a mountain an aggregate of these units; so in aesthetics, the intuition-expression is the unit, and such a massive and complex aesthetic object as the Rheims cathedral an aggregation of them. Such obvious differences as appear between the peasant-woman's outburst at King Alfred for burning the cakes and Thomas Hardy's epic-drama *The Dynasts* Croce seems to reduce to variations of mass and distribution. The woman's exclamation is a single aesthetic cell, or nearly so, and *The Dynasts* is a large number of cells. It doubtless requires greater concentration of attention to follow the configuration of the group than of the primitive and single form, but an increased measure of attention and patience is called for rather than a finer sensibility. As works of art differ in extension only, so the souls of men differ merely in the frequency with which they tend to express themselves lyrically. It is a mistake to suppose that there are artistic geniuses on the one hand, touched, as we enthusiastically say, with fire from heaven, and ordinary mortals on the other, who have no part in their gifts and happy fortune. "Great artists are said to reveal us to ourselves. But how could this be possible, unless there be identity of nature between their imagination and ours, and unless the difference be only one of quantity?"[17]

Judgments of the bare existential form, There is a work of art *a,* and, There is not a work of art *b,* are not isolated phenomena in Croce's philosophy, but are, on the contrary, typical of his method of constituting the universe. It would seem that for him not only is the world of beauty a universal without species, but that all the realms into which he divides reality are analogous abstractions. If he identifies two things, he treats them as absolutely coincident, and not as alike by virtue of some common character. They are one and the same, and that is all that can be said about it. Or if they differ, they differ absolutely. He realizes that if he treated resemblances between things as ideal identities of meaning instead of as quasi-spatial coincidences, the very foundation of his method would be immediately shaken. Thus he carries through his separation of identity and differences with an instructive ruthlessness. "People speak," he says, "of taste without genius, or of genius without taste. These . . . observations are meaningless, unless they allude to quantitative or psychological differences. . . . To posit a substantial difference between genius and taste, between artistic production and reproduction, would render both communication and judgment alike inconceivable. How could we judge what remained external to us? How could that which is produced by a given activity be judged by a *different* activity?"[18] For Croce an absolute choice is always forced: either two things are mutually exclusive entities (the partiality of quantitative coincidence does not affect the principle) or they are two in no logical sense whatever. For Hegel, Croce says, "the artistic activity is distinguished from the philosophical solely by its imperfection, solely because it grasps the Absolute in sensible and immediate form, whereas philosophy grasps it in the pure element of thought. *Which implies, logically, that it is not distinguished at all.*"[19] The notion that for thought a totality claims unity not by the exclusion of differences, but through their mediation, is foreign to Croce's mental habit, although he talks of syntheses and of identities in difference. There is for most of us more unity in a room—to use a homely example— which expresses its individuality through harmony rather than through bare sameness of color, and through the mutual adaptation of the forms of furniture and hangings to each other than through the absence of distinctive fittings.

The point of interest here is how difference of function may reinforce unity of meaning, so that the whole and part meet through some typical, ideal character. Resemblance to be resemblance must be distinguishable into the two moments of identical intent and difference of manifestation.[20] But for Croce, let there be the merest shadow of affinity between two things, and the likeness must either be interpreted as illusion or must push forward into absolute coincidence. "An activity whose principle depends on that of another activity is effectively that other activity, and retains for itself an existence that is only putative and conventional."[21]

It thus appears that some of the characteristic positions of Croce's aesthetics derive their quality from a logical method which fails to knit together in any concrete fashion the one and the many. Variety within his world of beauty is of two sorts. It is either absolute difference: the work of art is then unique, untranslatable, and incomparable; or it is quantitative: an artist's soul is, so to speak, more densely packed with unique expressions and utterances than the common man's. In so far as instances of beauty fall under the first head and are simply themselves and nothing else, they are beyond apprehension. That is, individuality which excludes ideal connections and the reference of the qualities and characters of its substance to species, is outside the pale of intelligence. To say that the manipulation of material, the choice and blending of colors and sounds, the rhythms and balance of patterns, or sublimity, in the sense of the overcoming of a peculiar recalcitrancy in the elements taken up into the whole—to say that these aspects or attributes or species of beauty have nothing to do with the success of the total effect is to fly in the face of facts. Croce almost accepts this extreme consequence of his reasoning, and lets the facts as such go when he is enlarging his theory, but fortunately, he is not altogether consistent. But in so far as he makes beauty both the utterly unique and also the intelligible and re-instatable, he combines two ideas which, as ideas, are irreconcilable.

In so far as beauty falls under the second head, that is, is expressive of quantitative difference, he seems also to be inconsistent. The point is, on what score is Croce entitled to any criteria of comparison at all? Grant him his abolition of all mechanical classifications and ratings—every philosopher worthy the name finds this a commonplace. But on his hypothesis of art as pure spiritual activity, as unique utterance, one wonders how he is entitled to even such a tenuous connection of content as the geometer's. For with a general relationship once admitted within the confines of beauty, the substantive nature has accepted as adjectival a definite analyzable aspect of reality which shapes itself in scientific generalizations, and the dogma of the merely intuitable many is gone. Moreover, quantity is a category to which Croce is in a special sense not entitled. For he regards the realm of body and space as an abstract construction of physicists designed to explain and subordinate to our practical ends our ordinary experience. But it is strange to fall back upon a practical abstraction to elucidate the principle of difference in the 'very real' world of beauty. How can one spiritual vision be more spread out than another? The term extension is intelligible in relation to the embodiments of the artistic impulse—there are longer and shorter poems and larger and smaller canvases—but Croce explicitly excludes these physical differences from the essence of beauty. In a word, it is only through space that Croce can explain the differences between the individuals of the universal Beauty, and yet the peculiar form of his aesthetic idealism which makes the intuition always disembodied spirit precludes his right to use that principle of individuation. Logically his one and his many must forever dwell apart.

There has been no attempt to deny in this discussion the suggestiveness of many of Croce's insights into the nature of beauty or the validity of many of his isolated assertions. But he furnishes us a collection of aperçus and images rather than a system of ideas. If "philosophy, like all other genuine sciences, has passed beyond the stage of the merely striking or suggestive treatment of problems, and aims not at interesting or picturesque results, but at the systematic organization of the facts with which it deals according to some general principle,"[22] then Croce belongs rather to the company of those who make the world interesting than to the company of those who satisfy the mind's demand for intelligibility.

V

SANTAYANA'S DOCTRINE OF AESTHETIC EXPRESSION

> Forms whose gestures beamed with mind.—Shelley, *The Revolt of Islam.*

Since the term 'expression' is the watchword of Croce and his disciples, and not only of these but of others who in certain respects differ widely from Croce, the connotation of the term in any considerable philosophy of the beautiful becomes a matter of primary interest. If in any given system the word does not serve as an alternative designation of beauty itself, it probably at least names one of the chief characteristics of beauty. Here then an inquiry into the meaning of a word tends to widen and deepen into the orientation of an aesthetic. Santayana's is such a "considerable philosophy of the beautiful," for he has a wide following not only among professed philosophers and psychologists who merely contemplate what they do not execute, but also among the exacting practitioners of the arts themselves, who quote his utterances approvingly in their critical writings.[1] Moreover, in his theory the conception of 'expression' does function crucially.

It is well-known that Croce makes art and expression coextensive: "Art is perfectly defined when it is simply defined as intuition."[2] "To intuit is to express; and nothing else (nothing more, but nothing less) than to express."[3] Bosanquet also stretches the term to the full compass of the theme of aesthetic: "To say that the aesthetic attitude is an attitude of expression, contains I believe if rightly understood the whole truth of the matter. . . . [Expression is] the keyword to a sound aesthetic."[4] And the doctrine of empathy—"the most commonly accepted of our time"—is based on the belief that a physical object may 'express' the inner psychical activity of a percipient. Santayana separates himself from all these interpreters at one stride by making expression, whatever he may mean by the term, not the whole but a part of aesthetic effect. For him it is only one of the three elements which combine to form the objectified pleasure which is beauty. The three constituents are, he says: (1) material beauty—sensuous imagery, vital feelings, simple colors and sounds and complex organic reverberations and reactions; (2) formal beauty—the arrangement of the sensuous and vital elements in pleasing shapes and patterns; and (3) expression, the quality acquired by objects through association, an associated value, the survival in presentation of the intent of a previous experience. Expression thus appears as a superadded charm; it is "the suggestion of some other and assignable object, from which the expressive thing borrows an interest."[5] The material and formal beauties of objects are, so to speak, dream-wares, utterly absurd and unmeaning from the standpoint of the logical understanding; expressive beauty has meaning; it "springs from beneath the surface," and is a "nether influence."[6]

In the first place, then, aesthetic expression for Santayana is a part of beauty rather than a synonym of it. In the second place, this part seems to possess a quality and origin, and therefore an individuality, of its own. It seems to be a distinguishable aspect or face of beauty and yet indeed to be more than this. At times it seems to have some capacity for existence over against its companion parts. Normally the three aspects are found together. But the objection to isolation of the parts would seem to be empirical only, not logical. To be sure, Santayana sometimes treats the parts as excisions

SANTAYANA'S DOCTRINE 117

and discriminations within a total content.[7] But the spirit of his whole philosophy is opposed to the notion of the logical compulsion of one term by another, and he does not appear persistently to imply that the matter, form, and expressiveness of beauty are bound to appear in conjunction. He says, it is true, that aesthetic effect has no parts when truly apprehended.[8] But in spite of this assertion, we shall see that he so treats the three elements that they seem to have the power of functioning independently; the flavor of each seems to remain whole and unimpaired in the ripe mixture; no one part seems to be transmuted by the others or by the whole.

Concrete examples of the parts of beauty subsisting by themselves support the hypothesis that the words "excision and discrimination" as descriptive of matter, form, and expression have a relative and not an absolute force. We are told, for instance, of a landscape whose beauty is expressive only. If the landscape has pleasant associations for us, we may feel in the contemplation of it a "deep and intimate charm," however "empty and uninteresting" it may be in itself. "We shall be pleased by its very vulgarity. . . . The treasures of the memory have been melted and dissolved, and are now gilding the object that supplants them; they are giving this object expression."[9] The glamor of this spectacle is then derived from something alien to the immediate stimulus of, say, brown uplands and ancient dwellings. If in other days I had not been happy amid these scenes—this particular animal I—then I should not now find it lovely. The same sensory material, with the same massing and focussing of color, might conceivably have left me cold. The beauty here embodied is the specific beauty of expression or association. As this is an illustration of beauty derived from expressive interest only, so cases may be imagined in which beauty is dependent on form and matter alone without the reinforcement of congenial imported significance. Expression may be absent from beauty as well as constitute its total presence and intent. An example would be a decorative inscription on a Saracenic monument as one who did not read Arabic might be aware of it.[10] Here the charm may consist wholly of rhythms of curve and color. The sound of Italian verse striking on the ear of a sensitive person who did not understand Italian would be a further example.

Beside cases in which one of the elements of beauty functions for the time being as the

SANTAYANA'S DOCTRINE 119

whole, Santayana gives instances in which, through looseness of structure, the sensuous and expressive content are, though both present, readily separable. This strengthens with fresh material the argument for the logically independent status of expression, and the presumption of the essentially fortuitous relation between expression and images. In stained glass, for instance, we have a "gorgeous and unmeaning ornament" which then "becomes a vivid symbol."[11] There exists for the sensibilities an expanse of rich color with "a look perfectly natural . . . a complete virginity of face, uncontaminated with the smallest symptom of meaning," to which, as a surplusage and like an afterthought, meaning may be added.

The independence of the expressive from the presentative element may even go so far, on Santayana's view, as to reach hostility. In tragedy, for instance, the effect of sublimity which is proper to that form of art depends on the capacity of an agreeable external show to conquer a horrible content. Here the two elements point in different directions; they only join after conflict. The tragic emotion is complex; it contains two contrary forces, for in this particular affective conscious process an element of pleasure must triumph over an element of pain. We must be at once saddened by the truth of the plot and delighted by the vehicle that conveys it to us. "A striking proof of the compound nature of tragic effects," he says, "can be given by a simple experiment. Remove from any drama—say from *Othello*—the charm of the medium of presentation; reduce the tragedy to a mere account of the facts and of the words spoken, such as our newspapers almost daily contain; and the tragic dignity and beauty is entirely lost. Nothing remains but a disheartening item of human folly, which may still excite curiosity, but which will rather defile than purify the mind that considers it."[12]

Without at this point prejudicing the issue of our argument, we may yet indicate for purposes of clarification that in any aesthetics of expression, conventionally so-called, this crucial experiment would be regarded as a monstrous proposal and as the *reductio ad absurdum* of the method that allowed it. Many philosophers would say that the supposition that you can abstract the medium from a work of art and have a recognizable part of it left is insecurely founded on mistaken theory. It would not be the story of Shakspere's *Othello*, or any component of it, so the argument would run, that would be left after the removal of Shakspere's verse and architecture; it might be—who knows?—such a scrap or theme as incited Shakspere to bring *Othello* into being, story and medium alike. But as in the finished play there are medium and plot which can no more be torn apart than the life of the blood from its substance in a breathing animal, so in the original slight hint that sets in motion the mind that makes the play there are the analogous two aspects. The true distinction, would be the claim, is not between a mass of sensuous imagery and its associated value, but between a slight form which clothes a slight meaning and a highly determinate form which clothes a highly individual meaning. In Croce's famous words: "Be it pictorial, or verbal, or musical, or in whatever other form it appear, [expression] is, in fact, an inseparable part of intuition. How can we really possess an intuition of a geometrical figure, unless we possess so accurate an image of it as to be able to trace it immediately upon paper or on the blackboard? How can we really have an intuition of the contour of a region, for example, of the island of Sicily, if we are not able to draw it as it is in all its meanderings? Every one can experience the internal illumination which follows upon his success in formulating to himself his impressions and feelings, but only so far as he is able to formulate them. Feelings or impressions, then, pass by means of words from the obscure region of the soul into the clarity of the contemplative spirit. It is impossible to distinguish intuition from expression in this cognitive process. The one appears with the other at the same instant, because they are not two, but one."[18]

In his conception of aesthetic expression, then, Santayana not only limits the term to a part of the aesthetic effect instead of expanding it into the whole, but assigns to this part a relatively high degree of self-sufficiency. We have seen that the plot of a tragedy is for him a constituent unmodified in its objective status by its way of appearing. A modification takes place surely, he would say, when a commonplace story acquires noble poetry for its vehicle; but the modification takes place in the individual consciousness of the observer, not in the substantial fact of the drama. The repellent quality of the tale is compensated for by the shine and artistry of the medium; but the tragic events are not themselves transfigured. Upon the view opposed to Santayana's this whole assumption of the separability of percipience and substantial fact in art is unwarranted. The story as finally expressed in the words of a master must be thought of as a new creation, not as the simple text which might have occasioned the act of creation.

But for a fair portrait of Santayana's theory his doctrine of the unity of artistic effect must be juxtaposed to his doctrine of the separability of functions. The two ideas cohabit, though they do not cohere. In his anatomy of aesthetic pleasure he confesses that he has done something that is dangerous and in a sense unsanctioned by the plain facts. In treating objectified feeling as if it were composed of parts, in distinguishing the material of things from the forms it may assume, and these from their associated value, he has followed, he says, "the established method of psychology, the only one by which it is possible to analyze the mind. . . . But aesthetic feeling itself has no parts, and this physiology of its causes is not a description of its proper nature."[14] Since Santayana himself recognizes the precariousness—even the measure of falsification—of his analytical procedure his own words furnish the stimulus for a critical consideration of his method and the inquiry as to whether any other approach to the aesthetic concept of expression may be less hazardous.

The central fact in Santayana's method for the critic is that in "following the established method of psychology, the only one by which it is possible to analyze the mind," he avails himself exclusively of the tool of history for the purpose of differentiation. "Expression," he says, ". . . differs from material or formal value only . . . in its origin." Physiologically and psychologically they are fused. "But an observer, looking at the mind historically, sees in the one case the survival of an experience, in the other the reaction of an innate disposition."[15] All three modes of beauty are blended in the act of aesthetic contemplation. But since the mediate value of beauty was—to borrow Alexander's terms—begotten by the temporal process upon space at a point-instant different from the moment of arrival of the immediate values, the two types may be treated as separate functions. The cause of associated meaning happened in creation's career before the cause of pleasant sound and pattern. Our writer's method then is to explain beauty by tracing the evolution of a content of experience, reporting how a particular complex has been built up out of elements through the operation of specific mechanisms. He conceives his task as an aesthetician to be the telling how charm and grace have been created, pieced together, erected. He focusses his search upon the primitive seeds and natural instrumentalities which in course of time conjoin to produce that arresting result—beauty. Being empirical-historical, his method will be observational rather than interpretative and linear rather than systematic. The reality of the temporal process and the validity of the function of sense-perception will be assumed. In the course of the chronicle there will be no inference to an element or force at work in the process which is not verifiable by reference to the ranging eye. The psychological reporter does not presume to guess what moves the world to individualize itself thus and so, but writes it off merely as it is given. "Here is an epic process, behold it," he seems to say. "Why it exists I do not know; but if it interests you, its course appears to be as I say." Any hypothesis of a *primum mobile* or a transcendent power, an immanent teleology or a soul or a pervasive divinity, is a gratuitous assumption outside the program of a scientific philosopher.

At first sight it would seem as if nothing could touch a description of this sort so long as it remained consistently untheoretical. A bare record of events is not a thesis to be supported or challenged. The disavowal of any intention of interpreting or adumbrating or divining ought, it would seem, to disarm the critic. But the ideal of a perfectly transparent report in the field of philosophy is a vain hope, and the notion of a detached observer who does not shape his history to the requirements of some assumption is a pretty fiction. 'Essences' which are merely 'intuited' and which are innocent of relevance, congruity, concept, or category, can only be conceived of by a violent effort of abstraction; and the 'facts' which a scientific aesthetic would recount actually swim in a context of opinion or conviction or supposition and cannot live and breathe outside their essential medium. So, in Santayana's case, the mere effort after transparency, the mere will to take events in the cosmic evolution as flat data, leads him, paradoxically enough, to an inclusive mental set. While explicitly intending abstinence from speculation, and while trying to report only what he has honestly seen with his eyes and heard with his ears, he ends by coloring his report with the

SANTAYANA'S DOCTRINE 127

prejudicial hue of fortuitousness. For chance is appealed to in his story, not provisionally and humanly, but finally and cosmically. There is thus a presumption of the accidental in his representation, and a postulate at the basis of his psychological aesthetics.

If anyone then undertakes to examine Santayana's transcript of reality in so far as it concerns the appearance of artistic species he will be struck by the frequency with which the category of sheer luck is invoked. A naturalistic philosopher, he tells us in his essay on Lucretius, substitutes law for fortune. But in his own naturalistic philosophy miracles and mysteries abound. The verbs by which he describes the arrival of new qualities in the world of art express accidental change rather than reasonable progression. For instance, this is his description of the emergence of beauty in human experience: "The ceaseless experimentation and ferment of ideas, in breeding what it had a propensity to breed, came sometimes on figments that gave it delightful pause; these beauties were the first knowledges and these arrests the first hints of real and useful things."[16] He here speaks of humanity "coming on" delight as we speak of the luck of sunny weather for a holiday. In describing the origin of dancing Santayana says that groping action passed into significant and disciplined performance by a "quite intelligible transition." Yet in stating this intelligible transition he asserts that conduct in the groping stage "lights on" its purpose.[17] In discussing the beginnings of music, our author considers the problem why a "pattering of sounds on the ear" should have as much moment "as any animal triumph" or "any moral drama." He says: "That the way in which idle sounds run together should matter so much is a mystery of the same order as the spirit's concern to keep a particular body alive or to propagate its life. Such an interest is, from an absolute point of view, wholly gratuitous. . . . We happen to breathe, and on that account are interested in breathing; and it is no greater marvel that, happening to be subject to intricate musical sensations, we should be in earnest about these too."[18] Apparently the basis of rationality on this view is the accident of a happy physiological organization. The account of the dawn of decorative art involves the same reference to fortuitous variation: "If [a man] happens, by a twist of the hand, to turn a flowering branch into a wreath, thereby making it

SANTAYANA'S DOCTRINE 129

more interesting, he will have discovered a decorative art and initiated himself auspiciously into the practice of it."[19]

There is a sense in which Santayana confines himself to the end to the principle of chance—if one may use so paradoxical an expression. For he assigns to that human faculty of judgment which turns back upon the train of existence, and endows it with import and value and beauty, only that same authority of spontaneous emergence which he gives to all other existences. Every impulse has initially the same authority as the censorious one by which the others are judged.[20] Yet to judge just means to apportion authority. How then can that which is without prerogative authority confer weight upon others? This perhaps is hardly Santayana's business to explain, since he is probably no more bound to justify justification than anything else. In the spirit of his system he might contend that the capacity of human reflection and art to enrich bare existence with relavance and harmony is a datum; that all the intellectual and aesthetic properties which are the outstanding attributes of the human world simply 'turn up.' Events so conspire, one might say, that reason attaches value to the blind impulse and the unprized apparition. Man "introduces consonances into nature" and so sustains what he doesn't originate. Life, we are assured, no matter how complex it may become, is at bottom pure feeling; yet this feeling may rise to such dignity that it is appropriate to say that it disciplines, orders, arranges, and rationalizes other and simpler forms of itself. Mental vegetation may so thrive and thicken that it may "gather and render back its impressions in a synthetic and ideal form."[21] Fitful nervous groping may so prosper that it can create symbols. Music starts with "explosive forces" that "loosen the voice," but these automatisms in course of time secure propitious retroactive effects, and presently a force is engendered which reins in and keeps from becoming vagrant the original sense-impressions. A capacity is generated which can control, reflect, and criticize, and which can develop style and taste. Human wisdom and power are, as respects origin, sediment of the flux of nature; but this sediment is unexpectedly precious and potent, for it proves to be able to fortify certain currents in the flux and cancel others.

Of course no one can disprove, in the mathematical sense, this report of the emergence of forms of art and qualities of being. On the whole the panorama presented corresponds with our inspection of the surface of cosmic history. And yet for a view that is designed to exhibit the hang of things—their connections and interrelations and significances—it leaves the reader with a curiously strong sense of disorganization and of appeal to the marvellous. The presentation seems alienated from its purport. Causes seem absurdly small in comparison with their effects. The accident of twisting a spray grounds, we are told, the superstructure of a decorative art. This announcement strains one's sense of credulity. An unmotived leap from chance gesture to self-conscious and complex world of beauty may have occurred in nature; but the apprehending intelligence finds it stranger that this should have been so than that it should not. Adequate cause for considerable effect is surely a postulate of all explanation. That the fortunate collision of pattering sounds with plastic sensorium should have engendered the intricate intellectual art of musical composition seems more like a guess calling for explanation than an explanation in itself. If indeed such a collocation of events is left at its face value and not further analyzed, it implies the unscientific notion, *ex nihilo multum fit*. Such value and import as natural events appear to the unsophisticated mind to carry bodily with them are, according to Santayana, imposed upon the events after the events by an effect of themselves. And in this the wonder lies: that out of the chance motions and clashings of primordial physical elements should issue massive spiritual capacities and centers of appreciation. We feel that the matrix can hardly sustain the offspring.

Such an ironical result is not out of harmony with the general tenor of Santayana's whole 'scepticism and animal faith.' The demand for logical intelligibility is in itself, to his mind, irrational. "The reason for my proclivity to play with ideas, to lose them and catch them, and pride myself on my ability to keep them circling without confusion in the air, is a vital reason. This logic is a fly-wheel in my puffing-engine; it is not logic at all."[22] Or if logic is not a fly-wheel in a puffing engine it is a "mere romance."[23] Certitude appertains only to the airy realm of essences, that is to merely presented contents untroubled by value or meaning; value and meaning are what arbitrary belief or interpretation adds by animal impulse.

SANTAYANA'S DOCTRINE   133

There is no such thing in reality as genuine logical constraint; on the contrary, the "real knowledge" which binds two things together is transitive and presumptive only; it is faith. It extends the jurisdiction of the mind from one thing to something alien, because its essential character is to mediate between two things which do not in their own right cohere. The ideal of rationality does not express a law of things but the accident of a creature's organization. "All theory is a subjective form given to an indeterminate material."[24]

In a theory which interprets rationality as a late and episodic birth of time and as a merely subjective phenomenon, it is not surprising to find that the ground and truest explanation of things is physical. "All origins lie in the realm of matter, even when the being that is so generated is immaterial, because this creation or intrusion of the immaterial follows on material occasions and at the promptings of circumstance."[25] In his concern not to "cut the animal traces" of spirit, Santayana almost leans backward and makes man effectively and for intelligence a biological subject, a kind of gifted brute. Life is for him an equilibrium of physical forces; the self a cycle of vegetative processes;

the ideal an emanation from the natural. Plastic art is really motor sensation. Spiritual facts are ultimately cerebral events. Space is the final category of intelligence. Specific values attributed to objects, such as colors and odors, are due to specific nervous processes. Inference is a feeling of relation. The love of nature is an overflow of sexual passion. Our impressions of the sublimity of the stars and of the Categorical Imperative are sensations of physical tension.

Santayana almost boasts indeed that he is a materialist. He would have the glory of being the only one alive. As, however, he immediately qualifies his boast by saying that he is not a metaphysical materialist, he takes the bloom from its cheek. If he means no more by the title than his willingness, "whatever matter be, to call it matter boldly,"[26] I scarcely see how he is to maintain his title against the most flouted idealist. For it is characteristic of the idealists to say with one of their leaders: "To reject the function of the body—our own and nature's—is not to honor but to bereave the spirit";[27] and with another: "Artistic fancy is always corporeal."[28] And yet there is truth in our author's boast. He not only assigns to matter validity, but primary validity; he not only attributes to it existence, but abstract existence. Other qualities of being come back to it as to a final resting-place; it is for him a latter-day first cause. For as we have seen, his method of understanding reality, at least artistic reality, is historical. The one sound analytical procedure was to spread functions and entities out in the order of their genesis. By this mode of analysis matter is primary; and mind, coming later, has to be superimposed on matter by an anterior operation. And the synthesis of the two seems more like a *mariage de convenance* than a union through affinity of nature and disposition.

There is then an immediate datum both in the history of the universe and in the aesthetic experience, and in neither case does the presentation carry its own intelligibility with it. Santayana's specific doctrine of the connection of presentation and expression in art by the fortuitous link of association is simply his whole system writ small. As in reality in the gross the psyche has to create spirit to bring into the cosmic process meaning and value, so in the aesthetic experience, the immediate imaginal content is forced to suggest for itself a logically alien import.

The alternative view is to take matter not as something which in its pure concept excludes mind, but as what it is understood to be, and sensation and fancy not as immediate data but as utterances. If the meaning of presentations may be taken as inherent in them instead of as "an ideal harness loosely flung over things," then the articulate grammar of both aesthetics and philosophy in general becomes less miraculous. For a speculative philosopher there is no problem in the 'compresence' of matter and spirit in the universe, soul and body in a biological organism, expression and matter and form in the sense of beauty, because in each of these essential coherence is taken as a birth-right. The so-called ideality of matter means for many idealists no more than that matter possesses a nature or intelligible character, this being an attribute over and above the capacity to stimulate an organism. Such philosophers find it rationalistic rather than observational to make matter originally and lumpishly physical and to exhaust the definition of 'things' in their relation to the sensorium. Since they believe that colors and sounds and fragrances speak a language in the very act of setting up nervous currents, they find it artificial to attach "associated value" to aesthetic presentation *post factum*. Beauty's expression is its nature. The thought of poetry, in poetry, is the music; sense and sound are a single compound life. Even in the test-case of elemental sensations—the splendor of red or yellow, the burst of a trumpet or the piercing tone of a violin—the sensation is felt by the human percipient not as sheer impact of ether-waves, but as utterance, that is, expression. Colors say something to us, though what they say cannot be translated into terms of ordinary discourse. If then expression is maintained to be innate in so-called pure sensation, by so much the more will it be innate in those examples of art which are more palpably representative or symbolical.

There is then nothing esoteric about a doctrine of aesthetic expression which holds that the ideality of art rests on a faith in the life and divinity with which the external world is informed, or that art adumbrates the divine attributes of nature. Such phrases as these, set in their complete context, imply the simple truth that art presupposes an import or expressiveness in all its objects, even the barest of them—

moreover, an expressiveness which is not appended to the presentation. Thus Santayana's remark that "there is no explanation in calling beauty an adumbration of divine attributes"[29] loses its sting. He has been misled by the figurative and enthusiastic language, and supposes there is vagueness because there is lofty metaphor. The truth of the matter would seem to be that there is more mystery in an aesthetic which simply allows beauty to graft itself on to data after the event than in one which holds that there is expressiveness and therefore beauty in sensation from its earliest dawn.

If proof were needed that the expressionism of the expressionists is a natural interpretation of artistic phenomena, such proof would seem to be at hand in Santayana's own naturalistic aesthetics. Though he affects a scientific attitude, and would gladly let all happen as happen will in a universe primarily composed of matter and moved by chance, he is at times decoyed by his imaginative gift into greater precision of perception. Witness his account of the "full vitality and music" of Lucretius' world. "We seem to be reading not the poetry of a poet about things, but the poetry of things themselves. That things have their poetry, not because of

SANTAYANA'S DOCTRINE 139

what we make them symbols of, but because of their own movement and life, is what Lucretius proves once for all to mankind. . . . Naturalism is a philosophy of observation, and of an observation that extends the observable; all the sights and sounds of nature enter into it, and lend it their directness, pungency, and coercive stress. At the same time, naturalism is an intellectual philosophy; it divines substance behind appearance, continuity behind change, law behind fortune. It therefore attaches all those sights and sounds to a hidden background that connects and explains them. So understood, nature has depth as well as surface, force and necessity, as well as sensuous variety."[30] It would seem from this that a natural philosopher divines directly the 'expressiveness' of nature. And all the "divine attributes" that a Platonist or Hegelian might desire are implicit in what this Lucretian acknowledges that he divines. The poetry of things themselves is the expressiveness of things themselves. If Santayana had followed the Lucretian argument whithersoever it would lead and had boldly ascribed movement and life to nature in requisite measure at all stages of her process, the difference between his interpretation and that of at least one critic would vanish.

VI

BEAUTY AND RELATIVITY:
THE THEORY OF CHARLES LALO

This universe . . . always was, and is, and ever shall be an ever-living fire, fixed measures kindling and fixed measures dying out.—*Heraclitus*.

Through nine brilliantly written volumes[1] M. Lalo has elaborated what he calls a "sociological aesthetic." He is not the first to treat beauty from the social point of view. As he himself points out, "sociological aesthetic, in spite of its air of novelty, is much more ancient than the words which designate it,"[2] beginning at least as far back as Plato and Aristotle. Yet the air of novelty is in a measure justified with Lalo for, departing boldly from the tradition of Taine in which he immediately stands, he attempts to socialize aesthetic values as well as the antecedents of artistic production. For Taine a work of art was a compound like sugar or vitriol; he aimed characteristically at nothing more than a descriptive science. Lalo, on the other hand, asserts that aesthetic is nothing if not normative. When he declares that "to think aesthetically is to think, at least subcon-

BEAUTY AND RELATIVITY 141

sciously, under the category of sociability," he means more than that the artist is soaked in his environment and limited by his epoch. He means that beauty, in the distinctive sense of its immediate address to the imagination, its compulsion of admiration, is also social.

Lalo's conception of aesthetic value presents itself to him as a mediation between two untenable extremes, impressionism and dogmatism. The thesis of impressionism is that the value of a work of art resides in the momentary mark it makes upon the individual consciousness. The worth of a poem or picture lies for the impressionist in the spontaneous and inconsequential response of the human organism. This isolated reaction may realize itself as a secondary work of art and thus become impressionistic literary criticism. But while such criticism gives *par excellence* the energy and charm of an artistic achievement, it possesses no scientific validity and pretends to none. Its force is rather that of autobiography or romance. "The good critic," says Anatole France, "is he who tells the adventures of his soul among masterpieces."[3] "Aesthetics rests on nothing solid," he says further, "it is a castle in the air."[4] Sainte Beuve called aesthetic impressionism "the Epicureanism of taste";[5] and little as he believed in its finality or trustworthiness, he yet wrote feelingly of the joys of the voluptuous and sensitive reader who inhales the finer breath of literary creation, and who only concerns himself with such aspects of art as tend to his delectation. The doctrine of the impressionists may be rendered as a paraphrase of the famous Sophistic utterance thus: "That is right in art which each man likes at the given moment."

Superficially taken, the thesis of dogmatism is the precise contrary of this. For the dogmatist, the value of art lies in the work itself, and is totally independent of any flux of impressions in sentient beings. Each example of artistic workmanship embodies, as it were, an aesthetic axiom, and commands with an underived authority. Thus dogmatic, for Lalo, was Plato's Idea of the Beautiful, and the academic Aristotelian tradition. But the most arbitrary aesthetic absolutes of all, he maintains, are the intangible emanations of French and German romantic genius. Even Brunetière, he says, the would-be Darwin of aesthetics, remained dogmatic, for while admitting the evolution of genres, he assigned an unvarying validity to principles of taste, and therefore made of particular epics or dramas scholastic entities and rational essences. For any dogmatist the rights of a beautiful object stand superior to the need of rational evidence or to the possibility of re-examination, but subsist by some mystical power of self-maintenance.

Both impressionists and dogmatists treat beauty as a value, and they thus share a point of divergence from the naturalist Taine. They are also subject to a common error: they give specific examples of beauty no intelligible grounding. They both place their theories beyond the pale of concrete criticism. A dogmatist, says Lalo, is merely an impressionist who arbitrarily exalts his preference to the level of universal reason. He formulates his conviction abstractly and then assumes it to hold for all minds and all ages. And the impressionist is merely a dogmatist who substitutes for Q.E.D. the words: "This is my good pleasure." His judgment is no less categorical. Lalo shares with both types of critic the insistence on value, but as over against both, he would rationalize the worth of art by reference to actual phenomena, and give a scientific sanction to the glamor of a lyric or a portrait or a fugue. His problem is to give a concrete and convincing warrant for the intuited authoritativeness of beauty.

He derives the clue for his own solution from within one of the rejected extremes—from impressionism. Impressionism, he says, is justified as a moment in the development of the science of aesthetics because it emphasizes the notion of relativity. For the notion of an 'absolute' is Lalo's ultimate abhorrence. Thus he says that LeMaître and France, in that they conceive of aesthetic worth as dependent on the reciprocal determination of objective stimulus and subjective receiving-apparatus and as varying constantly with the variation of either of these two terms, have made a genuine theoretical advance over their dogmatic opponents. If they could have carried out the implications of this insistence on relativity, he says, they would have arrived at a genuinely scientific doctrine. For it is the drawing out of the connections and relations of a work of art which settles the disputes about taste, and which gives the claims of concrete beauty more than a fleeting tenure. The relations of an aesthetic phenomenon to other phenomena function as the 'check' or 'control' on any expression of approval or disapproval concerning it. The organization of these relations becomes aesthetic law, a law which supplants the 'essence' of earlier theories. And this inductively supported generalization about a work of art replaces the fiat of a dilettante or academician.

What relations, then, are to be traced with a view to supporting or overthrowing the claims of any particular work of art? If the texture of relations is to be the check on the unsupported expression of taste, what is to be the check on the elaboration of relations? For the possible relations of any given phenomenon are infinite.

In his repugnance to arbitrariness Lalo accepts the only possible alternative to a definitive selection of pertinent relations. He will make no distinction between relations. He declares that what determines the value of a given work of art is the totality of its relations. "A complete scientific aesthetic," he says, "would be eminently relativistic because it would make the value of a work depend on the manifold relations between it and all other realities and all planes of reality."[6] "Aesthetic relativism," he writes again, in italics, "will only be complete when it has genuinely covered all relations."[7] Becoming more concrete, he specifies that aesthetic must be in turn mathematical or mechanical, physiological, psychological and sociological. And under sociological relationships he includes many types of connection, religious, economic, political, domestic. For example, in the investigation of the aesthetic value of a work of Palestrina's, its intervals would first be subjected to an abstract mathematical study in the Pythagorean fashion. Next there would be physical and physiological experiments in the manner of Helmholtz. Psychological interpretations of tones and scales such as have been made by Riemann, d'Indy, or Bourguès and Denereaz, would then be in order. And finally the polyphonic composition would have to be placed correctly within its social, religious, and technical milieu.

What strikes the reader in this description of method is no more the empirical stupendity of the requirement that all relations be traced than its unfortunate logical implications. An indeterminate universality tends to collapse both for science and logic into the opposite of universality—bare nothingness. If the conception of an unrestricted totality of relations is appropriate anywhere, it is in metaphysics. No doubt Tennyson's well-known apostrophe to the flower in the crannied wall involves a kind of theory of relativity. But it is not such comprehensive knowledge as Tennyson sums up in the phrase "what God and man is" that Lalo intends for aesthetic. Lalo is aiming at precise scientific results—knowledge comparable to the verified hypotheses of physics or biology. Now a scientific hypothesis can be verified only because certain precise conditions are laid down under which the investigation shall take place and because there is deliberate abstraction from everything that cannot be subordinated to these conditions. Certainty of result is bought at the price of limitation of the relations to be taken into account. For example, in Newtonian physics molecules are defined as qualified by mass, extension, and central forces proportional to mass. And certain equations and generalizations can be made on the basis of this initial hypothesis. But "the actual properties of molecules can only be expressed in terms of their potential orientations to various other kinds of molecules; and, when we pass beyond the comparatively simple empirical facts relating to crystallization, when we consider also the limitless empirical facts of chemistry, we can see that the physical conceptions of extension and central forces connecting masses are nothing but imperfect representations of reality, however useful these imperfect representations may be within certain limits."[8] Again physical chemistry, resting upon a definite conception of relations to be considered, allows very precise measurements to be taken of certain processes within the living body; but just because of its limitation of point of view, it cannot explain the active rôle that certain membranes in the body sometimes assume. In all fields the certainty of scientific result is consequent upon and proportionate to the quasi-artificial categorizing of the material in hand. If aesthetics is to become a science, as Lalo desires, then we ought to be able to discern an aspect of negation in its definition of method. But if, instead of this, we undertake scientifically to understand, say, a picture, and lay down no conditions, assume no working hypothesis, but take vaguely and grandly all relations of that picture for our province, then our method is not scientific but inappropriately metaphysical. Practically, all relations = no relations. Thus instead of progressing toward a concrete understanding of the aesthetic imperative we are back where we started from, in the *impasse* between impressionism and dogmatism and with no light on the problem of how the value of beauty is to be rationally supported.

Obviously, in practice, Lalo cannot hold to this all-embracing ideal of a complete web of relationships. Where there is no distinctness of approach there is no theoretical progress. Now there are different ways in which Lalo might give end and shape to his inquiry. He might, for example, limit the investigation of relations *intensively,* i.e., connotatively. He might start with some hypothesis as to the nature of an aesthetic object and treat the relationships under analysis as members of a specific kind of whole. Suppose, for example, he provisionally defined beauty as empathy or as significant form or as purposiveness without purpose, then his procedure would have definition. His general conception might or might not be retained, but at least it would serve as a useful temporary frame to limit his relating activity. At the worst, it would be a helpful heuristic device. Then, though mathematical and physical and religious matter might be introduced, it would only be introduced, as Spinoza says, *quatenus.* Some check would be operative on the measuring and the threading of connection, for measurements and threads of connection would only be considered in so far as they contributed to the elucidation of empathy or significant form or purposiveness without purpose. With the intensive limitation of relations the aesthetic object would be treated as an organic or individual whole, and some sense of the whole would operate in the research into detail of structure.

As a matter of fact, Lalo might well limit his investigation in this way, for in practice he has a restricted conception of the aesthetic object. Indeed, he fences aesthetic beauty around more narrowly than do many students of the subject. For instance, he has a principle on the basis of which he denies beauty to nature. The values of nature, he says, involve the categories of health, strength, type, sex, utility; the values of art those of the human surplusage of technique alone. Beside identifying aesthetic beauty with technique he defines it as the discipline of luxury, more specifically, as the socialization of erotic play. He disapproves, for example, of such a conception of art as that of Ruskin and Morris—joy in work. In explaining his theory of beauty as the discipline of sexual luxury, he says that the facts peculiarly sug-

BEAUTY AND RELATIVITY 151

gestive for the aesthetic inquiry are those relating to the family, the question whether the official regime in any country is polygamic or monogamic, the divergencies of law and custom on this point, the jealous cloistering of the harem, complete ignorance on a man's part of any women but his own, and on a woman's part of any man but her husband, such facts again as American, Anglo-Saxon and Scandinavian co-education, and the constant mingling of the two sexes in business and professional life.

Since Lalo busies himself through an indefinite number of pages in differentiating what he calls "anaesthetic" from aesthetic considerations, he would seem to have material at hand for a functional treatment of connections within an aesthetic object. And there are moments when he realizes that he must not leave his bundle of relationships lying loose and scattered like a chance assemblage of existences. He asserts, for instance, that none of the inferior planes of ideal organization—mathematical, physical, physiological—which condition the total effect of a work of art, imply an aesthetic qualification in themselves. He says: It is evidently not in the abstract that a concrete work of art reveals geometrical or arithmetical facts to us. These facts are relevant in art only as interpreted in the light of social discipline. They must somehow be absorbed into the social level. But I can never discover any elucidation of this movement of ascent, or any directing principle pervading it. He never seems to demonstrate how planes and lines and the balancing of forces are to be held always in control by reference to the individuality of the given technique or the particular instance of socialized sexual luxury, and I therefore tend to feel that Lalo is not in earnest with the organic principle of art which he adumbrates. The respect he pays to it seems to me largely verbal.

He does indeed make a slight destructive use of the principle of individuality in his criticism of the experimental aesthetic of Fechner and Külpe. Up to the present, he says, Fechner and his successors have only been able to use as tests of preference in formal beauty rectangles, ellipses, triangles, crosses, bisected lines, or lines followed by a dot like an *i*, or more complex patterns of points or areas or colors where the sense of symmetry is fostered or hindered by quantitative relations or equivalences of quality. He thinks highly of this type of investigation as a substructure to aesthetic, but he believes that the "atoms of value" thus established fall, strictly, below the aesthetic threshold. "This method," he says, "remains powerless in the exploration of concrete works of art, because no concrete work can be so simple as this, and such a work cannot retain aesthetic value when thus divided."[9] He compares Fechner's subaesthetic method to the preliminary chemical analysis of atoms of oxygen or hydrogen in the body, and he points out the difficulty of articulating the results of physiological chemistry with the concrete study of the functions of the lungs or stomach—functions which only exist in the medium of the totality of the organ. As the totality of the organ, then, acts as a check on the study of physiological detail, so the individuality of the aesthetic whole ideally pervades and directs the analysis of detail within it.

Thus Lalo verges on the enunciation of a functional principle by which he would limit the study of relationships. But he does not stand unambiguously for it, because he always suspects it of arbitrariness. He repeatedly insists that the genuinely complete aesthetic, the quite integral philosophy of the beautiful, will incorporate among its findings all possible relations.

A second possible way of making the study of relationships determinate would be by limiting them *extensively*. In this case a certain number of relationships would be cut off from the totality, and this class of connections would be identified with aesthetic value. Since this is a more mechanical mode of shaping the inquiry than the intensive method, and since Lalo prizes concrete rationality above all things, we would not expect to find him adopting it. Yet normally and practically he does define aesthetic value as one class of relationship—the social. "Aesthetic value," he says succinctly, "is glory or admiration."[10] What gives or denies to beauty a prerogative is the adhesion or repulsion of the social milieu—reputation, success or unsuccess, obloquy or ridicule. Only when a work of art is apprehended and appraised by a public does it cross the aesthetic threshold; before that it is the potentiality of beauty. Purely personal reactions are arbitrary and inconsistent, and cannot give a poem or a picture a status. In other words, until a work of art is confirmed and verified by the sign manual of a pleased constituency, it is an aesthetic hypothesis without objec-

BEAUTY AND RELATIVITY   155

tive validity. Social sanction confers authority upon that which without it would remain in the category of natural facts. That convenient instrument of speculation in all fields—the man on the desert island—could never create a true instance of beauty. He might fabricate in paint or marble and might like what he had made. But so may the fool approve his folly or the dreamer his dream. Imaginative constructs only attain the rank of value when their agreeable quality is ratified by the admiration of many. The universality which literary critics have ignorantly ascribed to particular works of genius sociological science now explains as unusual extent and persistence of social approbation. And the necessity of an aesthetic judgment, of which logicians speak, is, according to science, the substantiation given an individual preference by the coincidence of general agreement. "In that day," says our author, "when the public shall attach no superior authority to the name of Voltaire or Wagner, it will no longer be fitting to speak of the value of their works, except in an antiquarian sense. Their value would no longer be an actuality."[11]

The value of a work of art is, then, for Lalo, a variable, or, to adopt his own terminology, an evolving phenomenon. In respect to the sensible object it is an accident, like the moment of life which attaches to mortal clay and then departs. Homer's Odyssey had, for instance, its three-score years and ten of value, and then the value left it, like breath the body. Value is a fluctuating somewhat which now perches upon a design in paint or marble or language and now flies away again. It is not immanent in and specific to the aesthetic object. You cannot say it is *of* the picture in the same sense that you can say that the pattern or material is *of* it. The relation of value to art, on this view, is distinctly an external and occasional relation. Beauty happens to art, and is not one with it.

The social effects of a work of art form a texture, surely, which surrounds and sustains and in a sense places a work of art, and yet it is not quite clear why the consensus of these social effects should be a true judgment about an aesthetic object. The fact that Lalo takes into account various types of social sanction—the diffuse sanction of isolated individuals and the organized sanction of an academy or of an élite—that he identifies value not with the social sanction of any one generation but with the judgment which has survived many generations and has outlived conflicting prejudices—does not seem to alter the fact that he seeks to build up a universal out of an assemblage of particulars. The constant invocation of the word 'value' and of the descriptive term 'relativistic dogmatism' does not alter the radical empiricism of the method. Lalo does indeed recognize that the mere number of votes does not make art great. He says that the value of a work is proportionate to the "character of obligation, moral pressure, authority, or superiority" which derives from the living organization of the social body. But I cannot discover that the nature of this pressure is philosophically analyzed. I cannot attach any meaning to this consensus of opinion as value, unless I take it as psychological value-feeling. Then indeed we might have a description of the motivation for a particular act of admiration, but, so far as I can see, no justification of the admiration. The value-feeling would reveal itself as the aura of emotion of social sanction, the increment of sentimental force and vividness given to an opinion when it is sensed as one with the general opinion. But while this feeling of oneness with society does give a subjective impression of validity, it tells nothing about logical evidence. One may have a very strong sentiment that one is right, and yet by all disinterested standards be wrong.

If then, following Lalo, you say that for universality of art should be substituted more modestly collectivity of taste, you are in need of some canon of criticism for the collective taste. You need some principle of control for the relevancy of the social estimate. What counts is the qualified audience. But what constitutes qualification? Competence cannot be explained by further social approval, audiences appraising audiences *ad infinitum*. The minute you speak of qualification or competence in an audience you refer the whole question of the value of art back to the object. The society which confers distinction upon a poem is a society which can only be defined by reverting to the poem. Only those who have immersed themselves in the individual pattern and intention of the poem are entitled to pass upon it. Audience and object thus reciprocally determine each other. Value is, in a sense, a social fact, but it is not luck, which success often reduces to, but objectivity, that is, superiority to accidental and private significance.

BEAUTY AND RELATIVITY 159

It is the more surprising that Lalo does not distinguish between the relevant and irrelevant social reverberations of art since he is at great pains to distinguish beween the relevant and irrelevant pre-conditions of artistic creation. His chief animadversion against previous sociological aesthetic is that it failed to draw a clear line around the causes which were exactly pertinent. In the eighteenth century l'Abbé Dubos, he says, elaborated the influence of climate upon genius, but meteorology, he is careful to remark, is extra-aesthetic. Comte and Proudhon, he tells us, reduced art to something other than its distinctive nature, something economic, political, or scientific. In *L'art et la vie sociale* Lalo, like these earlier sociologists, presents anaesthetic conditions of artistic production, the economic, political, religious, and domestic determinants. But what they did in ignorance, he does self-consciously. He knows that in this volume he is working in the borderland of aesthetics and not in its proper domain, and because he is guided by a clear recognition of the method of his investigation he claims for himself transcendence of the earlier point of view. To attach art to the anaesthetic functions of society is necessary, he says, but dangerous. Only when a sociological aesthetician confines himself to the psycho-physical syntheses which are peculiar at once to sociology and to aesthetics, and which are irreducible to simpler data—in a word, to the evolving techniques and sanctions described in the history of art—does he in the proper sense cultivate his own garden.

In view of this neat cleavage between types of cause relevant to art and those not relevant, it is incomprehensible why Lalo does not sort out the analogous two classes of effect. There are psychological consequences appropriate to the peculiar constitution of a work of art, and there are those which fall beside the point. There are impressions of beauty which contain value and impressions which are valueless. There are socially impregnated reactions which are worth reckoning with and those which should be ignored. Lalo furnishes us no instrument of selection among these except the unavailable ones of "largest possible quantity of relations" and of immediate value-feeling.

The bulky *corpus* of Lalo's achievement is highly suggestive because he carries farther than anyone else has yet done the method of relativity as applied to the aesthetic object. He stands at the opposite pole from and challenges comparison with those writers who deny that a work of art has, as such, any relations at all. But if our examination of his arguments is sound, he does not convincingly demonstrate how out of a complex of purely empirical relations—however subtly they may be multiplied and woven together—may be derived the essential note of beauty.

REMARKS ON THE UGLY

It is now taken as aesthetic innocence to apply the word 'ugly' to the portraits of wrinkled old women, cacophony in poetry, discords in music, angularity in drawing or roughness of dramatic utterance. The shrinking from complex and uningratiating representation, if there is something powerful offered, is imputed to the timidity or intellectual narrowness of the spectator. But the new attitude raises a problem. If you extend the term 'beauty' beyond the mere easily agreeable so that it will include everything that is in any sense aesthetically moving, how much territory do you leave to the ugly? The tendency is to say, 'nothing.' Just as it is said regarding morality that "tout comprendre, c'est tout pardonner," so it is said of the world of semblances that to take in any presentation adequately involves giving it a positive worth. This, Saintsbury says, is the spirit of the new literary criticism. Your new critic "must constantly compare books, authors, literatures indeed, to see in what each differs from each, but never in order to dislike one because it is not the other." And Bosanquet with all his austerity and insistence on distinctions of value admits that he is much inclined to the view that there is no such thing as invincible ugliness. An appearance that is fully expressive of *anything,* he says, becomes *ipso facto* a kind of beauty.

The problem is one of extreme difficulty. On the one hand it is true that there is almost nothing which obstinately refuses to yield aesthetic enjoyment to one of sufficiently catholic imagination and with historical training. On the other hand, it seems as if to blot out the idea of ugliness altogether would be dangerously to deny a plain and pervasive indication of human feeling. Is it not rather, we argue to ourselves, that ugliness has been clumsily defined than that it does not exist?

If there is a region of the ugly, we might look for it either in a collection of instances, or in a principle which is nowhere entirely incorporated, but which fights against the spirit of beauty within particular appearances. Most people have their individual abhorrences in the realm of color. I believe that among the mature and sensitive there is a fairly general dislike of strongly-saturated pink. I know, for example, of an artist who is made physically ill by the sight of this color. And the same class of people would, I think, usually condemn the common Sunday-School hymn not merely from the religious point of view, but aesthetically. But it is hard to think of cases which have no gleam of aesthetic interest whatever, or which cannot be imagined in some setting that would redeem them. Put your revival hymn in a drama of negro life, and it may contribute markedly to the total expressiveness of the play. And one who dislikes the color pink in the abstract may admire it when it appears in a picture of fruit-blossoms.

The minute you begin to ask why you dislike particular colors or sounds, or dislike them in certain contexts and not in others, you abandon judgment on the basis of given empirical entities and begin to search for a principle of ugliness. Why, then, should the pure color pink and the undramatized Sunday School song have the tendency to offend sensitive taste? Is it, perhaps, that there is in both instances a spirit of pretense—a gesture of assertion which the substance of the color or the song cannot justify? Is pink a hue that is trying obviously to be a pretty color, and not resting content with simply being a color? And is it too feeble to support its claim? And is "Let a little sunshine in" trying to be religious music and failing in the effort? Is there the suggestion of solemnity without dignity, and of gaiety without sprightliness?

In such instances the fault seems to lie in the cleft between pretension and performance. One thing is aimed at and announced, another is achieved. A second kind of dissonance, aesthetically unpleasant, is that caused by the self-conscious cleverness of the artist obtruding between spectator and object. You are so distracted by the performer's demonstration of his dexterity and straining for effect that you cannot lose yourself in the contemplation of the object. Take the sentence from a contemporary English novel, a novel on the whole skillfully done but at the same time marred to my mind by self-consciousness: "He liked being told not to get his feet wet (in rain a butterfly would not have winked at)." Or this: "He had not previously discovered the Dutch garden, but it was a pleasant covert, at need, surrounded by spice-scented yew-hedges with caves in them; its centre-piece spurting with flower-flames, and pricked by the noses of many bulbs." Here it seems to me the metaphors get out of hand and call attention to the ingenuity of the author.

Too ostentatious a handling of medium in any of the arts may seem to interfere with and besmirch the presentation.

You may synthesize these two types of ugliness under the common idea of presumption, the presumption either of a sense-element or sense-complex or the presumption of a maker of artistic forms. Or you may root them both in the formal principle of incoherence. It does seem at times as if integrity of impression were the single *a priori* law of beauty. Of course no theorist can dictate beforehand how that integrity of effect shall be obtained—into how much variety the unity may be differentiated, into how much width the texture may be stretched, how any detail or element is to make for the whole. There is no rule for the way medium, mood, technique, idea, inspiration shall join their powers. But they must all join somehow. If any one element stands out as if by nature not to be fused through the efficacy of a presiding feeling, then it seems to me you have an infraction of beauty. I do not know to what extent for an ideal reader the long sermon in *Tristram Shandy* would be, throughout, contributory to the whole. For myself, I begin to feel ere long "preached at," and my enjoyment is temporarily under eclipse. Whether I am in this case a weak spectator or not, the principle is suggested by the instance. And those who feel that the red of the sail in the St. Frideswide window of Christ Church, Oxford, overbalances the rest of the window are controlled by the same principle of integrity of impression. Any insurmountable or unmotivated dissonance—between pretension and fulfillment, artist and product, or detail and totality—seems impossible to justify.

NOTES AND REFERENCES

I. Current Tendencies and Problems

1. *American Journal of Psychology*, XXXV, p. 407.
2. *Journal of the Barnes Foundation*, II, 1, p. 29.
3. *Vision and Design*, p. 301.
4. *Ibid.*, p. 82.
5. *The Principles of English Versification*, p. 12.
6. "Time in English Verse Rhythm," *Archives of Psychology*, May, 1908, pp. 10, 11.
7. See "Affective Sensitiveness in Poets and Scientific Students," *American Journal of Psychology*, XXXIV, pp. 105, 106.
8. Ray M. Simpson, *American Journal of Psychology*, XXXIII, pp. 234-244.
9. *Op. cit.*, p. 289.
10. "Recent Work in Experimental Aesthetics," *British Journal of Psychology*, XII, 1, pp. 81-90. Also C. W. Valentine, *The Experimental Psychology of Beauty*, pp. 27-34, 77-83.
11. XXXVII, 2, pp. 233-237.
12. J W. MacKail, *The Life of William Morris*, I, pp. 311-315.
13. J. W. Cross, *George Eliot's Life as Related in her Letters and Journals*, III, pp. 302, 303.
14. Warner Brown, *op. cit.*, p. 20.
15. *Op. cit.*, p. 10.
16. R. C. Givler, "The Psycho-Physiological Effect of the Elements of Speech in Relation to Poetry," *Psychological Monographs*, XIX, 2, p. 3.
17. Helge Lundholm, "The Affective Tone of Lines," *Psychological Review*, XXVIII, pp. 59, 60.
18. W. Van Dyke Bingham, "Studies in Melody," *Psychological Monographs*, XII, 3, p. 41.
19. *Op. cit.*, p. 11.
20. *Op. cit.*, pp. 89, 88.

NOTES AND REFERENCES 169

21. *Op. cit.*, p. 302.
22. *Ibid.*, p. 182.
23. *Ibid.*, p. 185.
24. *Ibid.*, p. 15.
25. *Ibid.*, p. 185.
26. *Ibid.*, p. 181.
27. *Ibid.*, p. 185.
28. Nitze and Dargan, *A History of French Literature*, p. 705.
29. W. H. Hadow, *Music*, p. 235.
30. *Loc. cit.*
31. Buermeyer, "Pattern and Plastic Form," *Journal of the Barnes Foundation*, II, 1, p. 27.
32. *Op. cit.*, p. 215.
33. *Ibid.*, p. 216.
34. *Ibid.*, p. 295.
35. Buermeyer, *op. cit.*, pp. 26, 27.
36. *Op. cit.*, p. 287.
37. Clive Bell, *Art*, p. 210.
38. Roger Fry, *op. cit.*, pp. 295, 296.
39. *Ibid.*, p. 302.
40. George Santayana, *Reason in Art*, p. 17.
41. Buermeyer, *The Aesthetic Experience*, p. 70.
42. *Thought and Things*, III, "The Springs of Art," p. 212.
43. "Genesis of the Aesthetic Categories," *Philosophical Review*, XII, p. 7.
44. *Op. cit.*, Appendix B, "Darwinism and Logic: A Reply to Professor Creighton."
45. Buermeyer, *The Aesthetic Experience*, p. 173.
46. Ritchie, *Darwinism and Hegel*, "Origin and Validity," p. 14.
47. "Genesis of the Aesthetic Categories," *Philosophical Review*, XII, p. 12.
48. *Sense of Beauty*, p. 211 ff.
49. *Ibid.*, p. 56.
50. *The Aesthetic Experience*, pp. 80, 81.
51. *Aesthetic* (trans. Ainslie, 2nd ed.), p. 14.

52. R. G. Collingwood, *Outlines of a Philosophy of Art*, p. 17.
53. *Op. cit.,* p. 13.
54. *Op. cit.,* p. 15.
55. *Ibid.,* p. 17.
56. E. F. Carritt, *The Theory of Beauty*, pp. 214, 215.
57. *The Theory of Poetry*, pp. 205, 206, 240, 241.
58. *Op. cit.,* pp. 212, 213.
59. *Ibid.,* p. 2.
60. Collingwood, *op. cit.,* p. 19.

II. Bosanquet on the Artist's Medium

1. He says, for example, that both Neo-Idealists and Neo-Realists assume that "the end is progress" and that consciousness is episodic; that logicians both of the type of Husserl and of the type of Spencer sever the ideal from the real and ultimately rest their theories on the same psychologism; that preoccupation with weakness or littleness in humility is like preoccupation with goodness or cleverness in vanity, etc.
2. The example is borrowed from A. C. Bradley, *Oxford Lectures on Poetry*, pp. 20, 21.
3. *A Defense of Poetry*, Ginn and Co., 1903, p. 7.
4. *Three Lectures on Aesthetic*, p. 52.
5. *The Distinction between Mind and its Objects*, pp. 24, 34.
6. *Three Lectures*, pp. 15-17.
7. *Mind and its Objects*, pp. 24, 25.
8. *The Value and Destiny of the Individual*, p. 79. Bosanquet suggests a possible qualification which is not here relevant.
9. Quoted by Bosanquet, *Mind and its Objects*, p. 7.
10. *Ibid.,* pp. 32, 33.
11. *Three Lectures*, p. 62.
12. *Popular Lectures on Scientific Subjects*, Appleton, 1873, p. 88.
13. *Collected Works*, XXII, pp. 182, 183, in the essay on "Some Hints on Pattern-Designing."

NOTES AND REFERENCES 171

14. *The Breviary of Aesthetic*, Rice Institute Pamphlet, II, 4, pp. 260, 261.
15. See S. Alexander, *Art and the Material*, pp. 15, 16, who makes the same point in considering Croce.
16. *Works*, 3, p. 332. "An Apology."
17. "Croce's Aesthetic," *Mind*, XXXIX, pp. 214, 215.

III. BERGSON'S PENAL THEORY OF COMEDY

1. Bergson, *Laughter* (trans. Brereton and Rothwell), p. 7.
2. *Ibid.*, p. 58.
3. *Ibid.*, p. 197.
4. *Loc. cit.*
5. *Ibid.*, p. 198.
6. *Ibid.*, p. 135.
7. Quoted by Philippe Legrand, *The New Greek Comedy* (trans. Loeb), p. 24.
8. *Euthydemus*, 273, 274.
9. *Laughter*, p. 6.
10. W. E. Henley, *The English Poets*, Selections with Critical Introductions, ed. Ward, II, p. 399
11. *Op. cit.*, p. 163.
12. *Ibid.*, p. 199.
13. *Lectures on the English Comic Writers*, ed. Hazlitt, "Shakespeare and Ben Jonson," p. 44.
14. *Oxford Lectures on Poetry*, "The Rejection of Falstaff," pp. 262-3.

IV. THE ONE AND THE MANY IN CROCE'S AESTHETIC

1. *The Theory of Beauty*, 2nd ed., p. 256.
2. *Aesthetic* (trans. Ainslie), 2nd ed., pp. 67, 68.
3. A. C. Bradley, *Oxford Lectures on Poetry*, p. 24.
4. Quiller-Couch, *Studies in Literature*, first series, p. 82.
5. *Op. cit.*, pp. 204, 205.
6. *Aesthetic*, p. 90.
7. *Breviary of Aesthetic*, p. 267.
8. *Ibid.*, p. 247.
9. *Ibid.*, p. 248.

172 STUDIES IN RECENT AESTHETIC

10. *Op. cit.*, chap. IX.
11. *Ibid.*, p. 255.
12. *Ibid.*, pp. 256, 257.
13. For an able defence of logical definition in literature see "The Validity of Literary Definitions," by Charles E. Whitmore, *Publications of the Modern Language Association of America*, XXXIX, 2, p. 722.
14. *Aesthetic*, p. 92.
15. *Breviary*, pp. 301, 302.
16. *Aesthetic*, p. 79.
17. *Ibid.*, p. 14.
18. *Ibid.*, pp. 120, 121.
19. Croce, *Saggio sullo Hegel*, quoted in Bosanquet, "Appendix on Croce's Conception of the 'death of Art' in Hegel," *Proceedings of the British Academy*, IX, p. 20.
20. I am much indebted throughout this discussion to the chapter on "The Theory of Association of Ideas," in F. H. Bradley's, *The Principles of Logic*, 2nd ed., I, pp. 299 *seq.*
21. *Breviary*, p. 273.
22. J. E. Creighton, "The Nature and Criterion of Truth," *Philosophical Review*, XVII, p. 593.

V. Santayana's Doctrine of Aesthetic Expression

1. For example, Quiller-Couch in *Charles Dickens and other Victorians*, pp. 55; "Academy Notes," The Buffalo Fine Arts Academy, September 1907, p. 68.
2. *Breviary of Aesthetic* (trans. Ainslie), Rice Institute Pamphlet, p. 250.
3. *Aesthetic* (trans. Ainslie), 2nd ed., p. 11.
4. *Three Lectures on Aesthetic*, p. 33.
5. *The Sense of Beauty*, 1896, p. 85.
6. See *Scepticism and Animal Faith*, 1924, pp. 137, 138.
7. See *Sense of Beauty*, p. 76.
8. *Ibid.*, p. 267.
9. *Ibid.*, pp. 194, 195.
10. *Loc. cit.*
11. *Op. cit.*, p. 76.

12. *Ibid.*, p. 226.
13. *Aesthetic*, pp. 8, 9.
14. *Op. cit.*, p. 267.
15. *Ibid.*, p. 195.
16. *The Life of Reason. Reason in Art*, p. 16.
17. *Ibid.*, p. 41.
18. *Ibid.*, pp. 45, 46.
19. *Ibid.*, pp. 118, 119.
20. *Ibid.*, p. 169.
21. *Ibid.*, p. 39.
22. *Scepticism and Animal Faith*, p. 121.
23. *Ibid.*, p. 101.
24. *Reason in Art*, p. 128.
25. *Scepticism*, p. 109.
26. *Ibid.*, pp. vii, viii.
27. Bosanquet, "Croce's Aesthetic," *Proceedings of the British Academy*, IX, p. 12.
28. Croce, *Breviary*, p. 263.
29. *Sense of Beauty*, p. 8.
30. *Three Philosophical Poets*, pp. 34, 35.

VI. BEAUTY AND RELATIVITY. THE THEORY OF CHARLES LALO

1. *Esquisse d'une esthétique musicale scientifique*, Alcan, 1908.
   L'esthétique experimentale contemporaine, Alcan, 1908.
   Les sentiments esthétiques, Alcan, 1910.
   Introduction à l'esthétique, Colin, 1910.
   L'art et la vie sociale, Doin, 1921.
   L'art et la morale, Alcan, 1922.
   La beauté et l'instinct sexuel, Flammarion, 1922.
   Notions d'esthétique, Alcan, 1925.
   La Faillité de la beauté (with Anne-Marie Lalo), Ollendorff, 1923.
2. *L'art et la vie sociale*, p. 1.
3. *Introduction*, p. 206.
4. *Ibid.*, p. 208.
5. *Ibid.*, p. 201.

STUDIES IN RECENT AESTHETIC

6. *Notions*, p. 25.
7. *Introduction*, pp. 338, 339.
8. J. S. Haldane, "Are physical, biological and psychological categories irreducible?," *Life and Finite Individuality*, Williams and Norgate, 1918, pp. 20, 21.
9. *Notions*, p. 16.
10. "Programme d'une esthétique sociologique," *Revue Philosophique*, 1914, p. 47.
11. *Introduction*, p. 334.

INDEX

Abercrombie, Lascelles, 35, 36
Absolutism, of romanticism, 142; Lalo's dislike of, 144
Agreeableness, sensuous, distinguished from aesthetic value by Fry, 17, 23
Anaesthetic values, distinguished from aesthetic by Lalo, 151
A priori principles in aesthetics, 16, 18, 166
Ariosto, 94
Artist, introspection of, 12
Artistic taste, objective validity of, 72
Association, psychological, aesthetic expression the same as for Santayana, 116-118
Assumptions, logical, of experimental psychology, 6, 7; of Santayana, 126 ff.

Baldwin, J. M., 27, 30
Barrie, James M., Sentimental Tommy interpreted as Everyman, 79
Baum, P. F., 5
Bell, Clive, 3, 4, 16, 21, 23, 24, 26
Blake, William, 21
Blueness, life of according to Bosanquet, 49 f.
Bosanquet, B., on artist's medium, 40-61; method, the presentation of a paradox, 40, 170; 92, 162
Bourguès, 146
Brown, Warner, 6
Brunetière, 142
Buermeyer, L., 3, 4, 31
Bullough, Edward, 9, 15; *a priori* principle in aesthetics, 18

Butler, Samuel, satire of *Hudibras*, 73

Cantle, Granfer, Hardy's character in *The Return of the Native* as comic hero, 87
Carritt, E. F., 32, 35, 36, 38, 89, 92; on the sublime, 97-102
Chance, appeal to by Santayana, 127-132
Classification in art, futility of in practice, 89; metaphysical implications of, 94-95; not philosophical according to Croce, 89; practical relevance of, 93; actual failure not decisive for logic, 96-97
Collectivity of taste, Lalo's substitute for universality of aesthetic value, 158
Collingwood, R. G., 32
Comedies, proportion of that are satirical, 68-70
Comedy, corrective function of according to Bergson, 66 ff.; characteristic effect of, 65, 66; incongruity of finite and infinite its ideal material, 88; ideal incongruities in, 84; interpreted as the negation of logical meaning, 83; commonly interpreted as satire, 68
Comic, bodily resonance of the feeling for, 62; Carritt's definition of, 39; relation of to logic, 62, 63.
Comparative greatness of works of art, problem of, 34-36
Comte, 159
Connotative method of classification in art, 100-101

Cowell, Henry, 11, 12
Criticism, growth of in experimental aesthetic, 9-12
Croce, on classification in art, 89-113; on physical basis of art, 112; on form and content, 121
Denereaz, 146
Dewey, John, 25, 26
Difference, absolute for Croce, 109
Discipline of luxury, aesthetic value defined as by Lalo, 150
Dogmatism, in criticism of art, 141 ff.
Dubos, l'Abbé, 159

Economic value, relation to aesthetic for Santayana, 31
Eliot, George, 11
Empiricism, Bergson's method in interpreting the comic, 63, 64
Evolution, in Lalo's aesthetic, 155-156
Experimental aesthetic, criticised by Lalo, 153. See *Psychology*
Expression, Croce's conception of, 115; crucial position of the idea in aesthetics, 114, 115; Santayana's doctrine of, 114-139
Extensive limitation of aesthetic relations by Lalo, 154

Falstaff, "absolute comic hero," 85-87
Family, important for aesthetics according to Lalo, 151
Form and content, in Croce, 121 f.; separable for Santayana, 120, 121
Formal beauty, defined by Santayana, 115 f.
France, Anatole, 141

Fry, Roger, 4, 8, 16, 17, 18, 20, 21, 22, 23, 24, 26
Function, aesthetic, how related to psychological "feeling," 12, 13

Genetic method in aesthetics, 25-32; limitations of, 30, 31
Glory, aesthetic value defined as by Lalo, 154

Hardy, Thomas, quoted, viii, 29; treatment of the comic in *Tess*, 75; Granfer Cantle in *The Return of the Native* as comic hero, 87
Hazlitt, on Shakespeare's comedy, 81
Helmholtz, on physical basis of harmony, 51-52, 146
Humor, allied to wisdom and religion, 88; implies social solidarity, 72

Impressionism in criticism of art, 141 ff.
Individuality of works of art, 90 ff.
d'Indy, 146
Instincts, of imitation and self-display for Baldwin, 27
Intelligence, ideal functioning of same as art, 28
Intensive limitation of relations of works of art for Lalo, 149, 150

Külpe, 152

LaFarge, John, 9
Lalo, Charles, sociological aesthetic of, 140-161
Laughter, social for Bergson, 71
"Laughter without offence," 71

INDEX

Law, aesthetic for Lalo same as essence, 144, 145
Leopardi, 33
Life, and mechanism in comedy, 64; continuity of with art, 26-34
Lucretius, 138, 139

Mallarmé, 20
Material beauty, defined by Santayana, 115
Materialist, Santayana a, 134
Matter, how related to spirit in Idealism, 136, 137; the physicist's philosophically interpreted, 46, 47; view of presupposed in theory of artist's medium as hindrance, 42-44
Medium, artist's, 40-61; regarded as impediment to expression, 41-54; regarded as outside aesthetic experience, 55-61
Meredith, George, The Egoist interpreted as Everyman, 79
M e t h o d, abstractness of Croce's, 110; current in aesthetics, 3-39; empirical of Bergson, 63, 64; empirical-historical of Santayana, 123-125; experimental, 6-16; formal, 16-25; genetic, 25-32; intuitional, 32-39; paradoxical of Bosanquet, 40, 170; normative-sociological of Lalo, 140.
Metrical rhythm and experimental psychology, 5, 11, 12
Milton, on relation of words to oratory, 58
Mind, the truth of body, 40; unpsychological connotation of for Bosanquet, 47, 48
Molière, 72, 74, 79

Morris, William, 11, 53, 54, 58, 150
Music, assimilation of arts to, 19, 20
Mysticism in aesthetics, 20

Nature, Lalo denies aesthetic value to, 150
Neo-Croceanism, method of, 32-39; logical rather than biological, 37, 38; tends toward negative and tautological judgments, 37-39
Newtonian physics, 147 f.
Nominalist, Croce a, 93; logical consequences of Croce's nominalism, 104-113
Normative, Lalo's aesthetics, 140

One and many, problem of in Croce, 89-113

Palestrina, 146
Panpsychism, Bosanquet's criticism of, 48
Pattern, distinguished from aesthetic form by Fry, 22
Physiological condition, relation to aesthetics for Santayana, 31
Pink, aesthetic quality of, 163, 164
Plato, 23; Ideas of, 20, 142
Poe, E. A., on composition of *The Raven*, 58
Primitive experience, affinity of art with, 33, 34
Proudhon, 159
P s y c h o l o g y, Experimental, method in aesthetics, 4-16

Quantity, category in Crocean aesthetics, 106, 107, 112

Reason, interpretation of by Santayana, 132, 133
Relativity, Lalo's aesthetic a doctrine of, 140-161
Rhythm, relation to labor, 31
Richter, "Jean Paul," 88
Riemann, H., 146
Ritchie, David, 30
Ruckmick, Christian, bibliography of rhythm, 3
Ruskin, 150

Sainte Beuve, 141, 142
Saint Frideswide's Window in Christchurch Cathedral, 167
Saintsbury, George, 162
Santayana, G., 25, 31; doctrine of aesthetic expression, 114-139
Satire, presupposes mutual exclusiveness of individuals, 70-72; transiency of, 73 ff.; its characters interpreted as types, 75 ff.; interpreted as a formal construction, 77, 78; interpreted as the limit of realism, 78, 79; affinity with cynicism and pessimism, 79, 80; dilemma regarding, 80; importance of fancy in, 81-83
Scientific certainty, conditioned by abstractness, 147, 148
Scriabin, 20, 21
Self-consciousness cleverness, element in ugly, 165
Shelley, on artist's medium, 42
Smith, J. A., 32
Social point of view in aesthetics, 140, 141
Song, problem of, 5
Subaesthetic method of Fechner, 153
Subjects, miscellaneous, in experiments, 7-12

Sublime, Carritt's treatment of, 99-102
Sunday-school hymn, aesthetic quality of, 164

Taine, 140, 143
Technique, aesthetic value defined as by Lalo, 150
Tennyson, 146, 147
Totality of aesthetic relations, Lalo's aesthetic ideal, 153, 154, 160; check on aesthetic value for Lalo, 145
Tragedy, how interpreted by Santayana, 119-121
Tristram Shandy, 166
Triumphant art, a problem for Neo-Croceanism, 34, 35
Tufts, James, 27

Ugly, 162-167; Carritt's definition of, 38; possible meaninglessness of, 162-163

Universal, art interpreted as the presentation of, 23, 24

Valentine, C. W., 9, 15, 18
Value, aesthetic, distinguished quality of, 17-25; exclusiveness of, 19; defined as formal relationship, 19; denied to be compartmental, 25; problem of its relation to continuity of life, 29, 30
Variable, Lalo's aesthetic standard a, 155, 156

Walkley, 32
Whistler, J. McN., 8
Whole and part in aesthetics, 13-16
Wilde, Oscar, 71

www.ingramcontent.com/pod-product-compliance
Lightning Source LLC
Chambersburg PA
CBHW030112010526
44116CB00005B/214